The Entrepreneurs Practical Workbook

(Guide on Getting Things Done)

(Shaf Cangil)

The Entrepreneurs Practical Workbook

Disclaimer:
Any and all advice given is to be taken at the discretion of the user and by using it, it is agreed that no Liability whatsoever is accepted by the author for any advice taken.

ISBN-13 978-1539548690
ISBN-10 1539548694

Dedication

I dedicate this Practical Worksheet to all brave entrepreneurs that have taken on the battle of working for themselves and accepted the challenge of creating their own little world to live, laugh and play in.

To all the teachers in the world that have worked tirelessly to make Practical Worksheets for their own subjects specific specialisms that help to do just that.

This book is to teachers that aspire to teach entrepreneurship
and to all entrepreneurs that aspire to teach.

The gap is closing.

Let us pick up the fallen and fight side by side.

The new era beckons.

Last but in no ways least, I dedicate this book to my dear cousin Erol Ahmet the gentle giant, whose presence will always be felt.
...Love you cuz. x

Footnote:
The Practical worksheets lean towards certain orientations like; detail (Steel), social (Blaze), creative (Dynamo), timing (Tempo) along with a fundamental WHY AM I DOING THIS? (Spirit).
These relate closely to Roger James Hamilton's Wealth Dynamic Profiles and he has kindly give permission for its logos to be used to highlight this.
You will find that certain days you can tune into one 'frequency' better than others but if you want to learn more then go to: https://www.geniusu.com/my-genius-test.

Table of Contents

Dedications ... 3

Introduction ... 5

Stabilising

Information Radiators ... 7

Current Mission Statement ... 12

Future Vision ... 20

Benchmarks and KPI's ... 26

Rewards Transparencies & Motivation ... 33

Soft Skills & Communication ... 38

Smart Goals, Prioritising and Mini Tasks ... 44

Agile Scrum Your Project ... 54

Productivity

Entrepreneurs Kick Off ... 62

Pricing ... 72

Hiring People ... 78

Forms ... 82

Decision Engine ... 87

Brochures ... 93

Processing Issues ... 104

Payment Issues ... 113

To Flow or Outsource ... 121

Planning an Event ... 128

E-Loyalty Cards ... 138

Collect & Categorise Your Assets ... 142

Automated Advertising ... 151

Our Thanks To: ... 157

Terms & Conditions ... 158

Meet The Author ... 159

Introduction

The goal of my book was to focus on a series of basic Practical Worksheets for entrepreneurs. Being a qualified teacher since 2007 and constantly in a circle of established business mentors (like Roger James Hamilton), the constant appeals on how to actually DO things as an entrepreneur spoke to me at a level that heralded these solutions.

Here's why they are now in a book for entrepreneurs to use...

Testimonials:

Ida Ahmet proprietor at www.bonniechic.co.uk

"OMG!!! You have blown me away! You have gone far beyond I ever imagined. This has put everything into order and for me to set goals. I am now able to move forward in my business plans. It has gone well beyond I imagined, without the techniques I've been given. I was just stagnating. It doesn't matter how much you already know. Sometimes a little help and a nudge is all you need. I originally had all these in my head, but wasn't able to get going as didn't know where to begin or how.

After speaking to you on Skype, I went away knowing you would be able to help and you sure have delivered a million times more than ever expected. I will be commencing first thing tomorrow morning and I already have my models ready for the photo shoots. Thank you so much for your help and support.

I would totally recommend Organisational Rescue!"

Didi Dimitrova Performance Consultant at DD Business Solutions Ltd

"OMG *Dear Shaf, you are just awesome! Thank you so much for preparing and sending this document to me. I am blown away of how detailed, directional and helpful it is.*

You are definitely getting free VIP tickets to my events for life!"

This book takes those very same Practical Worksheets, (adds a few more) so that any entrepreneur can now dip into what is in effect a manual, to ether refresh themselves on what to do or to actually to do things in a simplified effective manner in the shortest possible time.

Many thanks go to my associates that have kindly contributed with suggestions.

This book covers only some stabilising and productivity processes within a new business. It does not cover everything but it does use a very simple proven management method to help Identify, Analyse, Design, Develop, Test and Evaluate your steps.

Visit Organisational Rescues website for more. http://organisationalrescue.com/

This is The Systems Life Cycle which loops until perfection is achieved.

Being organised is the key. And I wish that for you.

Stabilising

In this section I have included areas that I feel lend themselves to stabilizing your business concerns. It covers a variety of practical tasks to follow that should be completed before endeavoring to move on to being more productive. Just as a tightrope walker should balance themselves before taking a step forwards, the stabilization stage is a fundamental sage to moving towards your goals.

Information Radiators

Blaze Energy Task
https://www.geniusu.com/my-genius-test

Objective:

1. To understand that transparency in the workplace gives value.
2. To create Information Radiators for use.

Identify

What is an information radiator and why would I need one for my business?

Transparency is the key to helping projects move forwards. It helps with communicating the status of a project to all and immediately display who is doing what at that time. Any issues that are causing issues or delays are immediately visible and how long it has been an issue can also be shown if dates are added to them.

Intervention strategies can then be added well ahead of the blockage getting too dangerous or more energy can be diverted to them to unblock quicker. Not only can the current state of play of the project can be seen but the speed of the project can also be calculated. This is useful to have when estimating deadlines and other metrics like quantity or quality. Even people outside off the project team should be able to read the information radiator so people joining the team are not put at a disadvantage and can contribute quickly. Duplication of effort is also avoided as each person will be in charge of something different.

Meeting times will be drastically reduced too as the team will be able to pick up each day with only a matter of minutes catch-up early in the day saving time and money and reducing the team going down the wrong direction.

Analyse

Information radiators can be any visual aid in a shared space. It can be electronic in nature if it is on a large screen but its best to opt for the least complicated option. A whiteboard or even a large wall expanse is fine as long as everyone on the team can access it at any time.

The update of this board relies on the whole team. Individual screens are not wise as the community that evolves around the one shared resource is also invaluable. Think of the many times teams have to come together and talk. They need to be frequent and as and when needed. Having a static board that is manually updated is also a kinesthetic activity that is enjoyed by many and offers a place to think away from the computer screen.

If you are working remotely make sure you have a slot each morning to just catch up and update it. We will cover this method later on.

Keep other valuable important relevant information there as well. Skills that people have or times they are not going to be available. Training they will need and even trips and rewards to the pub!

Have an area to celebrate achievements like completed training or fasted times or even family stuff that is ok to be shared like a new baby. This helps bring the team together and the value and support in knowing such things when humans are work on a project together is incalculable.

Design

Here are a few ideas for information radiators. Choose a style or add your own. Each should be updateable and clear.

- *Progress board (To do, Work in Progress, Done).*
- *Burndown chart (work completed over time)*
- *Backlog (Total workload/living document)*
- *Rewards and congratulations (Recognition and acknowledgment of effort/events).*
- *Training applied for/available (skills update on the way)*
- *Days not in (Teams can immediately see who's available)*

Develop

Make your own information radiators that you thing will help speed your projects up.

Amazon sells a fabulous whiteboard however a simple A4 sheet can also suffice if you have limited space!

Test

Take a week and use the information radiator in your workspace. See what works for you. Use it daily and fill in the evaluation sheet below.

Evaluate

Day	*Type*		
	Progress Wall chart	*Days off*	*Success/Achievements*
Monday *(Useful, Practical, unnecessary, hard to update, informative, valuable, will use again)*			
Tuesday *(Useful, Practical, unnecessary, hard to update, informative, valuable, will use again)*			
Wednesday *(Useful, Practical, unnecessary, hard to update, informative, valuable, will use again)*			
Thursday *(Useful, Practical, unnecessary, hard to update, informative, valuable, will use again)*			
Friday *(Useful, Practical, unnecessary, hard to update, informative, valuable, will use again)*			

Do you have any ideas for your own Information radiator?

How can you use it and what will it help with next time?

What have I discovered?

1. Transparency in the work place is of great value
2. I have a practical version of my own Information Radiators I can use.

ORGANISATIONAL
RESCUE

Current Mission Statement

Spirit Energy Task
Ying Yan fish designed by Organisational Rescue

Objective:

1. To understand the current mission statement for my business and projects and create relative stability.
2. To identify and apply 3 basic steps to my business and projects.

Identify

What is a mission statement?

Ok right about now you are saying, I am not a Space Program, I am not that exacting. I am just a business with a simple aim to make money and do a good job. That's great. You still need a plan of sustainable action.

For example, when you head out say, to the beach, you ignore the following?

- Where you are going?
- How long it will take to get there?
- Have you enough fuel to get you there and back?
- What if there's a roadblock or a strike (or other reasonable foreseeable problem?)
- What if the beach is too packed and you can't find a space?
- Who will come along?
- What provisions you will need?
- How much you will spend? (And THEN some!)
- What you will do there?
- What you might do AFTER you arrive and have spent the day?
- What effect this might have on people in the journey, around the journey and at the journeys end?
- What is the purpose of the beach trip?

Of course not. It's when we start thinking about what we do in other journeys that we realise that a business is a journey. In the next step we are going to break it down for you.

Remember, people that work for you and with you should have an idea of this mission statement so it needs to reflect your reason for getting up in the morning and working all day.

Just a little note here: You should already have specific goals for your business and you should be using them. As we intend to just stabilise your current business, your specific goals are not covered here. You will be looking at goals in your Benchmarking section but not here.

Analyse

Ask yourself:	*Translates as:*	*Organisational Rescue:*	*You:*
Where you are going?	***The direction of the company.***	*To provide help for entrepreneurs which are struggling to move forwards and are open to assistance.*	
How long it will take to get there?	***Your time period for results.***	*Helping 200 entrepreneurs in 12 months*	
Have you enough fuel to get you there and back?	***What is your financial situation and is it reasonably set up?***	*Part time work teaching and sales from consultancy with books and online courses.*	
What if there's a roadblock or a strike (or other reasonable foreseeable problem?)	***What contingency plans do you have in place for problems that you might come across?***	*Take on more part time work to fund the business.*	
What if the beach is too packed and you can't find a space?	***How will you deal with competition?***	*With my belief in my Unique Selling Point. That being a teacher and a business owner and having made many mistakes, I know what to avoid and what to do now and have a genuine desire to help those up and coming that should shine through.*	
Who will come along?	***What other companies or experienced entrepreneur groups can help you with your mission?***	*I have an extensive global network of established entrepreneurs that are always willing to share ideas and tips and share in the excitement of changing the world.*	
What provisions you will need?	***Resources, skills and experienced staff.***	*Skills include course creation for education and access to various online resources to deploy and share resources created.*	

How much you will spend? (And THEN some!)	***The budget you are allocating for this business.***	*TBA*	
What tells you that you have arrived?	***When you have achieved your goal how will you know?***	*Revenue through the business will increase and part time work can cease. Entrepreneurs will be sharing their experiences of the positive developments they have made through the experience. Links and Joint Ventures with other established companies arise.*	
What you might do AFTER you arrived and spent the day?	***The next steps your business might take.***	*Joint Ventures with larger establishments that help entrepreneurs.*	
What effect this might have on people in the journey, around the journey and at the journeys end?	***Benefits for yourself, staff and outsourcers and customers themselves***	*Feeling fulfilled and happy that the knowledge possessed and gathered over a lifetime is redistributed and targeted at the people that can use it the best to build a better world. That those contributing along the way also are spiritually enlightened and feel energised in sharing bet practices. Clients and customers know they are getting honest and tested ideas and help from other entrepreneurs.*	
What is the purpose of the beach trip?	***Why does this business exist?***	*There are too many people struggling to move forwards and this is impacting negatively on their family friends and health. In order to help them develop faster and even to exceed, it is right that everyone reaches out to pull others up when they can, wherever in the journey they currently are. This comes back a hundred fold when society learns to help each other and not just looks out for number one.*	

Design

Ok so it's time to see where you can train yourself, to stabilize your business through your mission statement.

Find a place to sit and think. Take your answers from the last section. We need to map your mission to what you are currently doing.

The more honest you are with yourself here the better. No one need see this but you. Look at your statements then answer the questions below. You do not need to answer them immediately. Better to read and think about the questions over a week then return with more clear solutions. Take those 3 at a time if you like. Remember there are no quick solutions. Allow your brain the time to link pathways and research during the week. Fill what you can and expect the answers to change when you know better. This is a living document. It never actually ends but it's got to begin, to work. Find the solution, do it, then train yourself to keep searching for better.

QUESTION	ANSWER	FOUND (Y/N)	DONE (Y/N)
What one tiny thing can you change that will make a massive difference in your current mission today.			
How could you increase your cash flow by two times in 6 months?			
What single thing will help you increase your personal wealth?			
Name 1 action that will improve your reputation drastically.			
Describe 3 small doable steps that make hundreds of customers come to your business.			
Who is the best partnership you can now connected with and why?			

What top 3 people can you hire to help you in your company now?			
Name the one little thing you can do to improve your health.			
What one basic action can lead you to a new beneficial network?			
Contact someone that you current see as your perfect mentor with a simple hello.			
Contact three affordable outsourcers that help your peace of mind this week.			
Consider 1 quick new skill you need to learn and learn it in a week.			
What one small course of action right now can help you manifest your mission?			
What 1 small thing will you contribute back this week?			
Name and thank the person you had to meet to avoid things getting harder at work and home.			
What simple 1 action will you adopt to			

motivate yourself over and over?			
What little free reward will boost you and your team?			
What single main limiting belief do you have and how can you convert it?			
What 1 simple little change did you have to do to make people believe in your dedication and help?			
Who must you listen to and who must you avoid on your journey that will make a difference?			
Add your own. The trick is to ask yourself a question that has value.			

Print out this document and add illustrations if you can. Some people prefer a vision board which they can look at. Some people prefer to read the document daily or weekly. Do not just create it and leave it hidden. Don't try to answer it now. Just allow the questions to sink in. It's a waiting game now. Choose around 3 or more to focus on that you feel are simple enough to do but powerful enough to make your business boom. Make sure to tick it off. Progress is in the ticks!

Develop

In order for you to generate some value here you need time. People tend to rush and fill in answers and hope that they will work then rush onto the next thing. My advice is to slow down. This is not a pop quiz. It's your business' life journey. You have time. These are massive questions that have been chunked right down into tiny motions so they are more likely to be done.

Imagine a massive ocean liner. It moves pretty slowly but it makes big waves. It has immense mass. It needs a lot of careful small adjustments to stay on course. One like adjustment can take the ship way, way off course of the captain is not careful. You have the time. You are not going anywhere that needs you as much as this does. Think and absorb, one at a time. Trust that one action to make a massive difference given time. Do it and then wait. Know that each solution is step and with time each steps answer will change too. Train yourself to watch out.

You may have heard of the law of attraction. Many right brained thinkers hold this to be true. On the other hand, the more left brained thinkers have heard about the reticular activating system in the brain. Whatever the case; it is very useful to have your brain trained to see solutions that it would normally not and this targeting of solutions is very powerful.

Test

I urge you to test each of the tasks I give you every time. It is important that these tasks make a difference for you. For some it will be a mind blowing experience and for others it will take more time and focus. Do not panic if you do not complete them all. This is a method to begin to move that massive ocean liner to stabilise your current business. There is no magic involved. It should provide the foundation of more ideas and thoughts and methods to balance your business as you go.

You can add some of your own too. Adapt the list to fit your business.

Evaluate

After a week ask yourself if you now have a mission statement that matches your passions regarding your business and projects and some small steps that you can implement straight away. Which are they and how does that make you feel?

What have I discovered?

1. I now understand the current mission statement for my business and projects and I can create relative stability.
2. I have chosen and will apply 3 basic steps to my business and projects.

ORGANISATIONAL
RESCUE

Future Vision

Spirit Energy Task
Ying Yan fish designed by Organisational Rescue

Objective:

1. To understand the Future Vision I am passionate about for my business and projects and create some actionable steps.
2. To identify and apply them to my business and projects.

Identify

Many if not all entrepreneurs have a Future Vision set in their minds already. This guide can only begin to introduce you to that vision however there are many other really useful resources you can use to get an idea of the fundamental Future Vision of your company and then you can build backwards from there.

'The Purpose Test' provides you with a simple quiz based on the United Nations 17 purpose streams that are focused around universal concerns from around the world.

To understand your own real purpose begin your adventure here http://purpose.geniusu.com/

A Future Vision statement is a short document that you write that will put down where you want your business to go in the future not why it currently exists (THAT is a mission statement).

You should share your vision with your team. This is important as teams can be a fantastic source of energy for you when times get tough. You may be surprised by where your next idea or help comes from.

From this point your projects and sub projects can be linked to the main vision to give a congruent feeling to your individual tasks and ultimate direction. Sometimes projects can come up that are challenging or nothing to do with your vision. It is up to you then to sit down and decide if this project is something you want to take on. That's up to you on an individual basis. Sometimes you will, sometimes you won't.

Analyse

Take some time and think about what you really enjoy doing and then consider the following:

YOUR FUTURE VISION:

- Your own personal values that energise you.
- What do you see around you and because of you?
- What are your new strengths?
- Do you feel stressed, obliged or frustrated when thinking about what you enjoy providing?
- Could it be of value to others?

- Can you identify 5 ways it is of value to others?
- Is it a sustainable direction?
- Are you aligned right now this this direction?
- Does this destination excite you in its entirety?
- Can you name the benefits and to whom?
- Would you enjoy the journey regardless of reaching the destination?
- Would you dedicate the time to it, whatever?
- When you talk about this direction do people comment on how excited YOU become?

Write down a future where you are living your dream and illustrate it with some images. Print out and stick on your bedroom wall.

Design

Ok, now time to capture some feelings and ideas that will manifest your Future Vision.

Find a new place to sit and think. Take a sheet of paper or open your notepad and take some time away from everyone to make your Vision statement. We need to harvest this vision's seeds.

Imagine you're 12 months in the future and you did what it takes to reach your destination already. Think, feel smell, touch, imagine the new world you are in and the people you have met, the kindness people have shown you and the doors that have been opened and those that could not just yet but will. As you sit in that neutral place (You could be in a hotel or a coffee shop but away from your current life) write as if you are explaining the past year and answer the following:

QUESTION	ANSWER	FOUND (Y/N)	DONE (Y/N)
What one thing did you change that made a difference in your journey towards your Future Vision?			
How will you feel when you reach your Future Vision?			
What single thing helped you increase your personal wealth?			
Name the action that improved your reputation drastically.			

Describe the steps that drew hundreds of customers to your business.			
Who was the best partnership you connected with and why?			
What top 3 people help you in your company now?			
Name the one thing you did to improve your health.			
What one action has taken you to your new network?			
Where did you finally find your perfect mentor?			
Consider the three simple steps that helped your peace of mind.			
Consider the new skills did you needed to learn and why.			
What course of action helped you manifest your purpose?			
What did you contribute back this			

year?			
Name and thank the things you had to do to make sure you did to avoid things getting harder at work and home.			
What actions did you adopt to motivate yourself over and over?			
What little free rewards boosted you and your team?			
What limiting beliefs did you have to eliminate and how did you do this?			
What did you have to do to make people believe in your dedication and help?			
Who did you listen to and who did you avoid on your journey that made a difference?			
Add your own. The trick is to ask yourself a question that has value.			

Print out this document and add illustrations if you can. Some people prefer a vision board which they can look at. Some people prefer to read the document daily or weekly. Do not just create it and leave it hidden. Don't try to answer it now. Just allow the questions to sink in. It's a waiting game now. The seeds you want are on the way.

Develop

For one week, read your Future Vision each morning first thing when you wake up. You will begin to remember each one. Allow your mind to absorb and consider each part. Do not skip anything no matter what. Do not force any answers. You may not have been exposed to any solutions just yet. You will know when you have. It's that simple.

Your brain will be forced to place these in its databank. The mind is very good at working out solutions even if they are real or imaginary. This is why we have presented it with some questions now so it has time to figure out solutions. Watch out for clues that may come your way well before they actually are needed. Like we mentioned before, some people believe in the law of attraction. Some people believe it's the reticular activating system in the brain, if it works then it's something you should consider.

Test

At the end of every day sit and consider if any of the 'seeds' have come up yet. If they have, capture them and write them down. They may be actionable solutions. If it feels 'Too rough around the edges' then give it more time. It will take time for the brain to find great answers. It's a long list. You can break it down to just one pre day of you like.

You can add some of your own too. Adapt the list to fit yourself.

Evaluate

After a week ask yourself if you now have a Future Vision that matches your passions regarding your business and projects and some seeds of ideas that you can implement straight away.

Which are they and how does that make you feel?

What have I discovered?

1. I understand what Future Vision matches my passions regarding my business and projects and I have some actionable steps.
2. I have chosen an appropriate Future Vision now.

ORGANISATIONAL
RESCUE

Benchmarks & KPI's

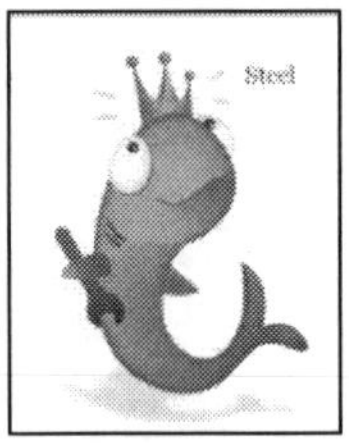

Steel Energy Task
https://www.geniusu.com/my-genius-test

Objective:

1. To understand what Benchmarks and KPI's are and their uses in projects.
2. To create my own Benchmarks and KPI's for use.

Identify

Benchmarking is an accepted level of progress or status that one uses to measure progress against.

Just as we use zero degrees centigrade to represent the point that water freezes and 100 at which it boils, you use Benchmarks to set the goals which you aim to achieve.

Find a similar company or business to yours and examine their Benchmarks (targets) if you can.

For example Polly's Perfume Counter has set a benchmark of £500 per day. Anything over this means they have exceeded their goals.

As a competitor you could then use their benchmark as your Benchmark to begin with. You then set your targets against these using SMART goals.*

If you excel a benchmark you are 'adding value' especially if Polly's Perfume Counter is a universally accepted benchmark by other similar companies or even highly recognised by your stakeholders.

You can use Benchmarks when building up your business plan to show your expectations over a period of time and also what you might put into place that would achieve and excel it.

Another phrase linked with benchmarking is KPI Key Performance Indicators.

These are your smaller milestones towards your ultimate Benchmark.

By keeping your eye on the KPI's placed along the way, you can adjust effort and energy towards your Benchmarks.

Analyse

Examples of Benchmarks can be, financial:

- £20,000 gross revenue to be made in 6 months from one product.
- Or service based:
- Less than 20 complaints about our total products per year.
- Or time based:
- Will not take more than 2 weeks to complete any project.
- Or comparisons to similar companies:
- This quarter we will match the sales figures of Polly's Perfume Counter.

You will notice that each target follows the S.M.A.R.T acronym *(Specific, measureable, achievable, realistic and timed).

Design

Find a quiet corner or go to a local coffee shop for some quality time alone. Take 30 minutes to think about the best key divers that really affect your business. Consider cash flow, sales, client turnover, likes on Facebook or any other measureable value you can think of that would make a real difference to your current project or business. (You have an example given).

My Benchmarks

Type (Cash flow, sales, client turnover, FB likes)	Specific (Method)	Measure (Number)	Achievable (Y/N)	Realistic (Y/N)	Time to achieve (No. of Mths/Wks/Days)
Sales calls	telephone	200 people	Yes	Yes	1 week (end of June 2017)

Develop

Here we will give thought on how these targets towards your benchmarks are to be achieved.

In order to move forwards one has to appreciate the starting position.

In any race, the starting point can be different per company just as the starting point of racers on a circular track may be different.

Let's give this some thought:

On a circular track, the innermost runners have much less distance to cover than the runners at the outermost track. If they were to all start at the same point and cross one finish line together, there would be an unfair advantage for the innermost runner. For this reason, the innermost runner is placed much further back than others to make up for the difference and so on for the other runners.

Life and business is very similar to this. You may feel that you are at a disadvantage by starting at a different point to others but this may not be the case. It is the distance or progress made that counts for a really profitable business and profit is the main reason for business.

Taking the list above you will now spend 1 week testing out ***one*** *of the Benchmarks.*

If you want to test out more you have been given more tables.

Use this table to track your ***Key Performance Indicators (example below)***

Benchmark	**Monday: Key Performance Indicator 1**	**Actually done:**	**Tuesday: Key Performance Indicator 2**	**Actually done:**	**Wednesday: Key Performance Indicator 3**	**Actually done:**	**Thursday: Key Performance Indicator 4**	**Actually done:**	**Friday: Key Performance Indicator 5**	**Actually done:**
Sales calls: telephone 200 people in 1 week to end June 2017.	40	20	40	24	40	15	40	55	40	28
Benchmark	**Monday: Key Performance Indicator 1**	**Actually done:**	**Tuesday: Key Performance Indicator 2**	**Actually done:**	**Wednesday: Key Performance Indicator 3**	**Actually done:**	**Thursday: Key Performance Indicator 4**	**Actually done:**	**Friday: Key Performance Indicator 5**	**Actually done:**
Benchmark	**Monday: Key Performance Indicator 1**	**Actually done:**	**Tuesday: Key Performance Indicator 2**	**Actually done:**	**Wednesday: Key Performance Indicator 3**	**Actually done:**	**Thursday: Key Performance Indicator 4**	**Actually done:**	**Friday: Key Performance Indicator 5**	**Actually done:**
Benchmark	**Monday: Key Performance Indicator 1**	**Actually done:**	**Tuesday: Key Performance Indicator 2**	**Actually done:**	**Wednesday: Key Performance Indicator 3**	**Actually done:**	**Thursday: Key Performance Indicator 4**	**Actually done:**	**Friday: Key Performance Indicator 5**	**Actually done:**
Benchmark	**Monday: Key Performance Indicator 1**	**Actually done:**	**Tuesday: Key Performance Indicator 2**	**Actually done:**	**Wednesday: Key Performance Indicator 3**	**Actually done:**	**Thursday: Key Performance Indicator 4**	**Actually done:**	**Friday: Key Performance Indicator 5**	**Actually done:**

Test

Take a look at the results of your experiment and think about the results. How could you use these values?

What could you say about each?

What actions could you have put into place and when and how can you improve next time?

Could you have thought of some actions and strategies **before** the numbers changed? What would that be?

Did you try any intervention strategies and did they work?

Evaluate

Do you feel that you could use Benchmarking and KPI's in your own business now?

What have I discovered?

1. Benchmarks and KPI's are essential if my key driver's progresses are to be monitored in projects.
2. I have at least one benchmark and a series of KPI's created for my own personal business project.

ORGANISATIONAL
RESCUE

Rewards Transparency and Motivation

Objective:

1. To understand what my business can do to reward and motivate people I touch transparently.
2. To create 2 ways that I can do this in my business

Identify

In any business or job, there is a transfer of energy and effort from one to another for a set value exchange, this is almost a given.

It may surprise you to know that this is not a motivator for work. It is an expectation. Expectations are the starting point for anyone that works with you.

Motivation is point where the exchange of value is tipped in the favour of one of the parties. Using motivation to stabilise your business can help reduce turnover of staff and even win you more positive attention overall as a caring business which is super awesome!

The mistake a lot of people make is that the belief is it has to be directly monetary. It does not need to be. There are many other ways that one can exchange value for effort and energy that is of great value but not money.

Google has the money to really go to town on this and it is linked to increasing productivity there. Ok so you don't have Googles budget, who does, so here's a few ways you might be able to adopt some 'Googlesque' techniques for a fraction of the cost, or for free.

Analyse

Here is a list of motivators that are not money related but very powerful nevertheless.

- Offer workers more control over workload

- 1 hour per week to do any project –linking to your business- and taking an interest in it.
- Dress up days (World Book day, Christmas, Easter) or a red t-shirt day in exchange for free coffee vends and best outfit on the office wall or intranet.
- A Friday kebab treat (Or Pizza, Kentucky, Burger, Nandos, Costas or Cosmos) day for everyone regardless of input.
- A wall board (Check out our stuff on Information Radiators) to display a leader chart of success (Can be work based or even the score of a weekly darts match)
- Darts match per week for 1 hour with teams. (Or trivial pursuits or even Kahoot (https://getkahoot.com/how-it-works) a virtual quiz game that can be globally linked and played) with team going on board as winners.
- An after work bowling, squash, cards, badminton team.
- Birthday cakes and tea/coffee/smoothies on staff birthdays for all.
- A suggestion box to contribute anonymous improvements to work and conditions. Then take one each week to trial. Adopt if agreed.
- Non-monetary based 'Thank You' cards (even electronic!) to those that have done overtime or exceeded their goals. A personal message from the boss can have a massive effect because thebe acknowledged for exceeding expectations can be awesome.

You can come up with similar list of fun relief that everyone can join in on as well.

Some of these can be directly productivity related because let's face it; you are not Google with an unlimited budget. However, always include some that are not in any way restricting to all. Everyone has something in their lives that weigh them down. It may be because of you, it may be from years ago that has nothing to do with you but when a business goes out of its way to share community and spirit, everyone troubles can go take a hike for 1 hour a week and THAT'S motivating.

Design

Take some time to design something that will work for your business and people that you associate with.

This can be workers, suppliers or even your customers and clients.

Don't be shy about thanking people around you. Sometimes a smile and a thank you can beak the mood cloud around someone's head and help them forget their troubles for a moment. That makes you a special person to be around in this world. People like to do business with a smiling face in front of them. Think about it. They say one random act of kindness is worth its weight in gold and can put someone in a good mood for the whole day.

Do it! It's good for you! It's good for them too!

Develop

Choose two ways from the selections above and then take this week to implement it. Use your own if you have one! Of course this will not work on all types of business such as outsourcing however even thank you cards can be a lovely way to show your gratitude and they are just as powerful as a real card to the brain as long as it was genuinely meant!

Test

To measure the effectiveness of your 2 motivational implementations you could use this simple feedback questionnaire or make one yourself with SURVEYMONKEY or Quick Surveys for free:

https://www.surveymonkey.co.uk/r/S8QR7XH

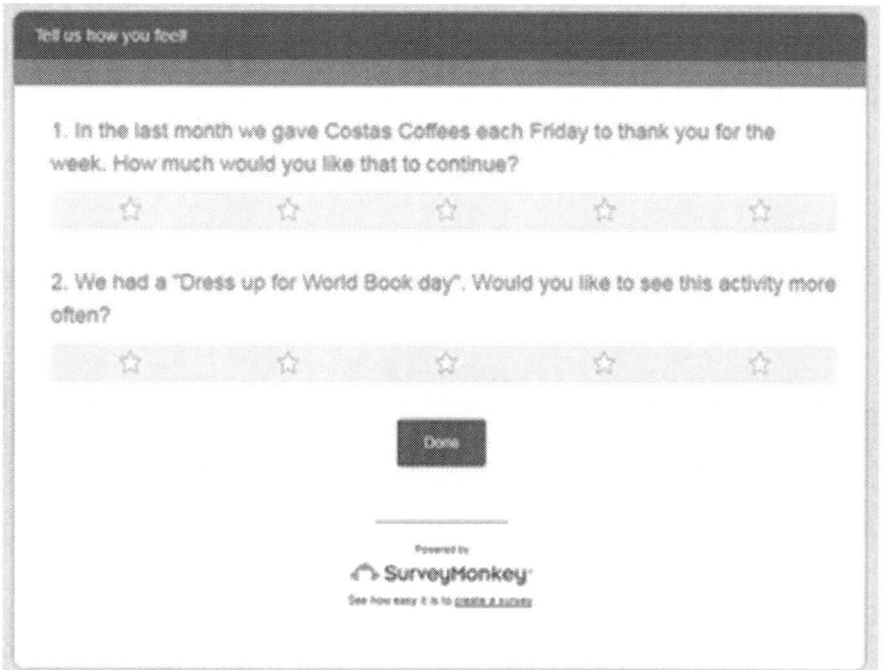

Evaluate

As ever it's important that you are implementing strategies that stabilise your working environment. In this case it is encouraging your staff to stay with you and others to realise you value people over and above their pay. Think deeply about the changes that you are witnessing and if they are sustainable. You can swap these around and see which works better and to make sure they are seen as treats and not expectations.

I used to have a boss that gave out ice lolly's each week on really hot days way back when I was a fine art watercolourist working next to a sun drenched window all day and that was super awesome. When they changed it for a trip to the pub, and bought us all gin and tonic, my 19 year old non-alcohol nature didn't really appreciate nearly as much!

If it doesn't fit the team or staff, it won't work so well! So: Explore and evaluate!

What have I discovered?

1. I understand what my business can do to reward and motivate people I touch transparently.
2. I have 2 ways that I can do this in my business

ORGANISATIONAL
RESCUE

Soft skills and Communication

Blaze Energy Task
https://www.geniusu.com/my-genius-test
© Wealth Dynamics
Replicated by kind permission of Roger James Hamilton

Objective:

1. To understand what Soft skills are and types of communication in business project management.
2. To know how to use each in a given scenario.

Identify

Being an entrepreneur running a project means having to improve on your soft skills communication. These are types of interaction that assist negotiations in business deals too.

In managing projects it is fundamental that you use the correct tone and visual clues that will encourage people to want to help your business and not build walls in your way instead.

Now you may have certain traits that are specific to you. You may be great at detail but less great at communication. We are not here to explain why this is. You can explore Gardner's Multiple Intelligences or Briggs Myers type indicator, Wealth Dynamics Profile or any other variation that can help you much more than this guide can.

However, having the knowledge of how these can explain where you stand on these skills, will allow you to understand how much effort you will personally need when running or being in a project.

Analyse

Email: Requires netiquette, a type of communication with rules such as:

- DO NOT USE CAPITAL LETTERS AS THIS APPEARS AS IF YOU ARE SHOUTING.
- Do not use exclamation marks for the same reason!!!!!!!!
- U shud not use txt msg shorthand.
- Use bullet points.
- Keep emails formal and short. Most people get so many emails and speed reading can cause upsets.
- Spellcheck TWICE then read it before sending

- Never send emails while you are angry or emotional.
- Do not use slang
- Use readable font styles. (Use readable font styles).

Telephone conversations, with no visual connection makes communication that much more difficult and communication can break down easily. Here are some top tips:

- Smile and sit up when you are talking. It comes across in your voice.
- Have a short list of topic you'd like to discuss and stick to it. Note down responses.
- Always ask if it is a good time to talk, Phone calls are usually interrupters and disruptors. If it's not, then book a better time. Then call then.

Skype: being face to face is a close match to being physically there however eye contact may be missing due to camera angles and lead to some interesting connections and understandings.

- Try to keep the camera directly in front of you to give a better sense of connection.
- Have a list of points you want to address and stick to them.
- Remember you are being watched so make sure you are not in unacceptable attire or state.
- Makes sure your room is well lit. There is nothing worse that talking to a shadowed outline.
- Have the camera at eye level. No one wants to sit and count nose hairs.
- Remember global time differences matter.

Listening face to face: in direct proximity is the most natural method however not always the best for all concerned.

- With introvert leaders this can drain their energy so brief limited contact that's to the point is better than long drawn out meandering monologues.
- If you find you are talking to someone and their eye contact disconnects, it's a fair bet you should conclude your point in summary and
- Ask if they have understood.
- Do not over touch unless you have (or want) that kind of relationship.

Talking face to face: The most natural method that can be used to show you are listening to a person is to

- Repeat what they have just said.
- Mention them by name and then ask them if you understood them and then simply repeat what they said.
- It is important to keep eye contact unless absolutely unable.
- The other person will feel listened to and most properly you will have time to take it in and are not rushing from one place to another.

Conflicts:

- The best way to handle simple conflicts is to
- Speak to each individual concerned independently and make sure they all are aware that this is taking place in confidence.
- Ask for an explanation of the situation but do not prompt or blame. Make notes.

- When each party has had a chance to explain then you can decide if this is a small matter that can be handled by yourself or a mediator or Human resources needs to get involved.
- If they are open to giving a solution that works for them, ask for this while you have them alone and then decide a best way forwards from what you hear.
- Explain the situation to both when they are together and explain that it is a professional workplace and that you expect professional conduct at all time.
- Do not raise your voice.
- Do not talk to anyone that raises their voice or shouts or used bad language.
- Model the behaviour you wish to see.
- Get in writing and sign off an agreement and result of further action that will be taken if this happens again making sure all parties receive a copy.

Moral building:

- A business has to have a vision. If your team on the project is feeling less than happy, you may need to remind them of the vision and make sure they are in tune with the outcome.
- Ask for the team to express themselves in their work even if they are outsourcers. It is important that everyone's input be noted and given due thought and consideration. You may take votes on outcomes or debate to include and welcome people initiatives. Eventually you find that they will come forwards with their own suggestions to save you money, time and effort which improves morale.
- Add some occasional treats unrelated to work that are unexpected and fun.
- Have a wall of achievements or have a weekly presentation for the best ideas of the week.
- Verbally thank people for their time and energy. It can be more valuable sometimes than money so make sure you do this visibly and sensitively as well.

Design

Take some time now to think about the areas above and tick each one that you feel would be useful to you or that you would like to explore further.

Write down 5 of the things mentioned above that you would like to investigate more here.

Area for investigation:	Applied to:	Result:

Develop

In the next week complete the table on the previous page and record your results.

Test

What aspects did you find were the most productive for you?

Try out another 5 next week and record the results. You should now have improved some aspects of your soft sill communications for your teams and projects.

Record them here:

New Areas for investigation:	Applied to:	Result:

Evaluate

Which techniques do you feel have added value and you will use from now on in your teams?

What have I discovered?

1. I understand what Soft skills are and how to use different types of communication in business project management.
2. I can choose an appropriate method of communication for a given scenario now.

ORGANISATIONAL
RESCUE

SMART Goals, Prioritising and Mini Tasks.

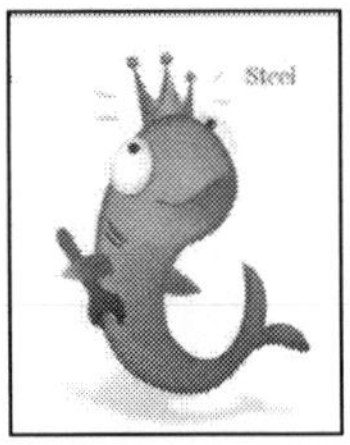

Steel Energy Task
https://www.geniusu.com/my-genius-test

Objective:

1. To understand that my current goals need to be verified and prioritised.
2. To create a list of verified and prioritised Mini tasks to stabilise my current position.

Identify

Have you sat down recently and looked at your current goals and duties and given them some serious thought?

In all fairness you may have started out with clear transparent sensible structured goals and along the way something happened and slowly but surely you find yourself meandering dangerously away from your initial intent?

A well-known method of goal setting is **SMART. Specific, Measureable, Achievable, realistic and timed**. Use this to verify that you are manifesting your vision and not just being busy for the sake of being busy.

Examples of goals could be:

- To have a 4 part mini online course about fly fishing, of 30 minutes per section in two weeks' time.
- Write a blog on the best locations you have fished in London by the end of today and get feedback or likes.
- Contact and submit an article about the latest fly fishing accessories to 3 professional fishing magazines, by the end of month
- Take 20 pictures of people fly fishing in London's top locations.
- Research the latest news on fishing tackle boxes online.
- Interview a fly fisherman's top 10 fly rods.
- Advertise your mini course in 3 professional fishing magazines.

When you have done this you will need to **prioritise them**. This is when you place each task or duty in logical order relative to each other and also with the most urgent to your stakeholder's, your cash flow and your vision. If you think of each as either important and needed ASAP that's a start.

Personally, it would make sense to look at cash flow as the most important of the areas mentioned. You can then place stakeholder's desires, and then your future vision.

Analyse

How can we map these into your reality?

The Eisenhower Decision Matrix

	Urgent	Non Urgent
important	*Now* *(Green)*	*Later* *(Yellow)*
Not important	*Outsource* *(Green)*	*Reject* *(Red)*

You may have seen the Eisenhower decision matrix (The above table is derived from it) but never known its name. This well-known grid is based on the 34th president of the USA (term: 1953-1961) Dwight D. Eisenhower: who was reputed to have said: "I have two kinds of problems, the urgent and the important. The urgent are not important, and the important are never urgent." From the above grid that was derived from that statement one can only assume that he had only tasks that could be outsourced or done later!

Where ever the grid comes from, it allows a method to prioritise and streamline tasks where you can find no other rule.

If we add a red amber and green traffic light situation to it you can see what needs to be done now by you or others, what can wait (whosoever does it) and what really need not bother you.

Let's apply the grid to the goals and issues above to get an idea of how this could work.

Time and sequence order is the key to placing tasks in the right box...

- To film a 4 part mini online course about fly fishing, of 30 minutes per section in two weeks' time.
- Write a blog on the best locations you have fished in London by the end of today and get feedback or likes.
- Contact and submit an article about the latest fly fishing accessories to 3 professional fishing magazines, by the end of month
- Take 20 pictures of people fly fishing in London's top locations.
- Research the latest news on fishing tackle boxes online.
- Interview a fly fisherman's top 10 fly rods.
- Advertise your mini course in 3 professional fishing magazines

	Urgent	Non Urgent
important	***Now*** *(Green)* • Write a blog on the best locations you have fished in London by the end of today and get feedback or likes. • Advertise your mini course in 3 professional fishing magazines	***Later*** *(Yellow)* • To film a 4 part mini online course about fly fishing, of 30 minutes per section in two weeks' time. • Contact and submit an article about the latest fly fishing accessories to 3 professional fishing magazines, by the end of month
Not important	***Outsource*** *(Green)* • Take 20 pictures of people fly fishing in London's top locations. • Research the latest news on fishing tackle boxes online. • Interview a fly fisherman's top 10 fly rods	***Reject*** *(Red)*

You can now place these in logical order in a timeline or calendar of events and carry them out knowing that they make sense when completing.

Don't forget, this depends on the speed of your business completing its tasks which can vary from company to company and team to team and person to person. This is covered later in SCRUM (Agile Scrum your project P 54).

Now

1 **Write a blog on the best locations you have fished in London by the end of today and get feedback or likes.**

2 **Advertise your mini course in 3 professional fishing magazines**

Outsource

3 **Take 20 pictures of people fly fishing in London's top locations.**

4 **Research the latest news on fishing tackle boxes online.**

5 **Interview a fly fisherman's top 10 fly rods**

Later

6 **To film a 4 part mini online course about fly fishing, of 30 minutes per section in two weeks' time.**

7 **Contact and submit an article about the latest fly fishing accessories to 3 professional fishing magazines, by the end of month**

Some people skip this step in the hope that they can just do things faster or are eager to get going hoping things will be clearer as they go. The old adage: "Work smarter not harder" will soon make itself felt if you try that.

It's best to take a little time and get this right so you can relax later on knowing that you have planned this stage correctly which reduces stress and allows for you to focus on giving value when executing.

I personally have to plan for 516+ kids for a 40 week period each year and this means multiple linked lessons that have to make sense have congruency and not feel disjointed. I can look at the time I actually have with them and then omit or reject areas that are not important or essential in order to fit the best stuff in.

That can take up to two weeks pure hard work planning researching thinking about content and relationships and timing and just plain common sense and by using the Decision matrix. I never start new tasks at the end of a term when the kids are winding down for a holiday and I never place a writing task before the kids have time to research. You don't have to prioritise and verify workload but if you really want to reduce stress, and improve productivity it's a jolly good way to go about it and I strongly advise it.

Design

Write down 20 SMART goals you have this month from big to small. Don't worry about the order. Just add the ones that come to you and make sure they are as small as you can get them.

You will know they are small enough when you think: "I could finish that in a couple of hours or so".

Try to chunk them into really tiny tasks. I call them 'Mini Tasks' for a reason. If they are too big, you won't even get started!

Here is a Decision Matrix for the next month. Take time to chunk down your goals into smaller parts until you have all your tasks placed.

	Urgent	Non Urgent
important	***Now*** *(Green)*	***Later*** *(Yellow)*
Not important	***Outsource*** *(Green)*	***Reject*** *(Red)*

Place your new order of tasks here:

	Task	Done (Y/N)
1		
2		
3		
4		
5		
6		
7		
8		
9		
10		
11		
12		
13		
14		
15		
16		
17		
18		
19		
20		

Develop

In the next week see how many of these actionable mini tasks you can achieve. Tick off each one as you go.

Test

After a week come back and take a real good look at the results so far. How do you feel you have done? Is there a better way for you to do each?

If you have to, redo the table and this time add tasks you know you can do, not impossible ones that you 'should' but can't! Keep chunking down and adapting them until you get a series of things you know you can and will do. It's not a matter of always going out of your comfort zone, there is quite a bit within your comfort zone you can do and do really well! Use that for now.

Evaluate

What other ideas do you have about using SMART goals, prioritising and chunking by yourself to realign your tasks now?

What have I discovered?

1. I understand why that my current goals need to be verified and prioritised.
2. I possess a list of verified and prioritised Mini Tasks to stabilise my current position.

ORGANISATIONAL
RESCUE

Agile Scrum your Project.

Steel Energy Task
https://www.geniusu.com/my-genius-test

Objective:

1. To understand the fundamentals of Agile Scrum and use them to run a project.
2. To adapt my own project to work with Scrum

Identify

Scrum is the name of a method used to run team projects that create a Minimal Viable Product. It takes its name from the Rugby term Scrum where the team huddled together over the ball to get control over it. Project Scrum was originally created for Software development teams however it base root style, called Agile, is also used to run various other types of projects non software related. Here we adapt SCRUM.

It all begins with a business having to create a product.

The person that deals with gathering requirements for the product is called a Product Owner. This person sits and talks with the stakeholders and builds a list of requirements to present to the team. The list is called a Product Backlog. It's a living document, which means it can be continually updated. This allows the 'ultimate' product to remain as fresh as it can be, at any given time so it's still marketable by the time it's completely finished.

Do you think this is a good way to keep up with the latest marketplace trends?

The team takes a look at the ever updated Project Backlog and along with the guidance of the Product Owner takes a snapshot portion of requirements that they feel can be built in a two week period. This means that a first stage version of the final product can be created which is as fresh and as close to what is wanted at the time and cannot be any more out of synch to the ultimate product than 2 weeks.

This is normally very attractive to stakeholders.

The Product Owner (you) secures a snapshot of work for the team. They also explain to the stakeholders that in 2 weeks' time, a Minimal Viable Product, MVP (Something that is basically sellable) will be created quickly for them. Any additional changes, adaptations and updates will then be done to that new creation after this point.

So work begins.

The team creates the MVP as fast as they can in two weeks.

When two weeks ends, the team with you, the Product Owner calls the stakeholders and presents the MVP.

The MVP requirements are checked off, payment can be made and if more updates are required to be added to the MVP from the Product backlog it can be agreed here.

After this, the team and Product Owner meet up to discuss any efficient ways of working next time. This is a Retrospective.

Let's say the stakeholders want more to be added. The Product Owner updates the Product Backlog again (Because business is ever changing) and then presents that to the team. They look at the product they created and how this can be moved forwards now with new updates.

By using this method, the latest MVP remains fresh and continually updated to provide the best fit to requirements.

Analyse

Examine what method your team is using now. They may have some of these techniques in place.

- Do not get caught up in software or ways used. There are many available and each are good in their own way however even a whiteboard and post it notes can be used for large companies and highly complex solutions quite well. As long as your team is happy, don't sweat it.
- Do not excessively worry about documentation over productivity. If you are building it and it fits the bill, keep documentation at a minimum.
- Do make sure you are fulfilling your customers' needs and providing the freshest version desired. Don't get too caught up in EVERYTHING the customer wants at stage 1. Be realistic as you need a MVP per 2 weeks. Business changes and that's life. That special function that makes tea via their mobile phone device can wait until the basic device is working first. Many times that new function will phase out as fast as it phased itself in any way!

- Keeping your customer happy means keeping their customers happy so everyone's happy.
- Do try and respond to the latest and freshest Product Backlog.

These rules are captured in the basis of the Agile Manifesto that underpins Scrum.
Here are some steps you should apply to your teams:

1. Do not exceed a maximum of 7 people in any one team.
2. They must all be in communication with each other
3. Preferably in the same room
4. Have multiple cross over skills that they don't mind doing, sharing or learning.
5. Have a visible Information Radiator to show important information instantly.
6. Do break down your snapshot of work into mini tasks that one person can do alone. Write each of them on a post-it note.
7. DO NOT assign tasks to individuals in the team. They have to choose their own tasks.
8. Display all the tasks on the whiteboard in a column called, TO DO. Have a middle column called, Work In Progress and a last column called, DONE.
9. Each morning have a 15 minute stand up meeting around this board and get each person to give 3 answers:
    a. What they have done
    b. What they are choosing to do next
    c. But what is holding them back from that.

   There should be one person that eradicates problems for everyone and keeps the ball rolling.
10. When each person has taken a note and moved it to the centre WIP section, date it. Let them go off and complete their task. When they do they can move the post it note to the DONE section and get another from the TO DO list. This continues all day. At the start of the next day, repeat the stand-up questions again and remove issues again. Repeat all steps for the 2 week period and then make sure you have a Minimal Viable Product created.
11. Have presentation to the stakeholder and Product Owner.
12. Have a Retrospective
13. Congratulate yourselves

Design

Here is where we apply the above to your own business.

If you do not have a team but are working with outsourcers you can use this just as effectively. If you are working alone don't worry, we all have and sometimes that's what we go back to. That doesn't mean you can't apply SCRUM and improve productivity.

Here's what to do now:

Write down all the requirements of one product you are responsible for making. Just add the lot. Don't do column 2. That comes later.

PRODUCT BACKLOG (REQUIREMENTS-ALL) BOOK PUBLISHING	CAN DO IN 2 WEEKS (MVP CREATION)

Awesome. That's your Product Backlog done!

Now you can go back and all you have to do is tick (or cross) the ones you think can get FINISHED in 2 weeks.

I mean a Minimal Viable Product. (Something you can charge for).In case you're not sure, it should look something like this:

Product Backlog (Requirements-ALL) Book Publishing	Can do in 2 weeks (MVP Creation)
Create a short book on how to create a website in 3 days.	x
Order proof copy	x
Start marketing it on social media (Hootsuite)	
Set Benchmark targets for sales and other KPI's*	
Adapt your marketing strategy	
Promotional videos.	

- Key Performance Indicators will be in another posting!
-

Here is a two week timetable. Break down those tasks into Mini Tasks. These are things that can be done in 1 day or less.

Get your team (or yourself) familiar with each aspect.

Add it to a timeline:

Here's one we made for our book story. Use the empty one next to it for your own.

1	DAY	DAY	Minimal Viable Product
2	1	Mon	*Research the subject matter.*
3	2	Tues	*Get title and front cover ideas for the book*
4	3	wed	*Find online self-publishing outlet.*
5	4	Thurs	*Learn how to self-publish on it.*
6	5	Fri	*Collect your raw material and images in a folder neatly.*
7	6	Sat	
8	7	Sun	
9	8	Mon	*Download a template and add the text with spell check.*
10	9	Tues	*Optimise images to 300 dot per inch (DPI)*
11	10	wed	*Add the images to the template.*
12	11	Thurs	*Upload and review*
13	12	Fri	*Add prices and distribution*
14	13	Sat	
15	14	Sun	

1	DAY	DAY	Minimal Viable Product
2	1	Mon	
3	2	Tues	
4	3	wed	
5	4	Thurs	
6	5	Fri	
7	6	Sat	
8	7	Sun	
9	8	Mon	
10	9	Tues	
11	10	wed	
12	11	Thurs	
13	12	Fri	
14	13	Sat	
15	14	Sun	

You should now have enough to begin work.
Remember to complete each mini task in a day. Cross off when done.
You can use a white Scrum board if you are a team.
Use a simple white sheet of A4 paper sideways if working alone.

Develop

You should now be able to use this to implement this action in your business.

Test

As in all my posts you have a chance to TEST the effectiveness of this action. It is important that you understand and grasp the fundamentals of the concept correctly and in his way realise your goals.

Look at your Product Backlog list. Can you cross off any of the Product Backlog after 2 weeks?

Evaluate

Here we can improve what happened.
Fill in the following:
What actions did you have put into place and when?

Could you have thought of some other actions before each task? What would that be?

Did you try any additional techniques and did they work for you?

What have I discovered?

1. I understand the fundamentals of Agile Scrum and can now apply this to a project
2. I have at least one project that has moved to a Scrum situation.

Productivity

ORGANISATIONAL RESCUE

Once the tightrope walker has found their natural balance it is time to move on.
Occasionally it is the forward motion that assists balancing, just like riding a bike.
This next stage helps some businesses to progress and stabilize as well. Pay careful attention to your cash flow at all times and remember to keep that work life balance in check.
Entrepreneurship is a marathon, not a quick sprint…

Dynamo Energy Task
https://www.geniusu.com/my-genius-test
© Wealth Dynamics
Replicated by kind permission of Roger James Hamilton

Entrepreneur 'Kick off' (Sonia Czernik Suggestion)

Objective:

1. To understand that my business ideas needs to be captured, solidified, packaged and *priced* in order for others to understand.
2. To capture, solidify, package and price my assets in my business.

Identify

Ok, now it's time to get serious. In this Practical Worksheet you will get an overview on how to organise your business idea and concept so that you have something at the end of the day that is recognisable as a standalone business and that can be easily understood by other businesses and customers. Your ideas may seem perfectly clear to you and indeed they are! However it's making them as attractive as possible to the customers and other businesses that you are stuck with right?

Business ideas occasionally become so overlapped with various ideas that it becomes difficult to explain to others in one breath let alone in an 'Elevator Pitch'. Don't worry. We have a plan that will begin to take you from here to there in clear easy to understand steps. For reasons that will become apparent this Practical worksheet can only cover the highlights. Look out for individual Practical Worksheets that link to these as our database expands or sign up for the 'Smart Charting' and 'Awesome Support' packages at the end of this Worksheet that break down your specific journey just for YOU.

So as a good start we will:

1. Capture your ideas,
2. Investigate the options
3. Collect and categorise your assets

4. Isolate your most likely Target Market
5. Map your best assets to your Target market
6. Check competition
7. Find your Unique Selling Point
8. Set your price structure
9. Get a timeline
10. Brand yourself
11. Address social media
12. Check out joint ventures and partnerships
13. Check out freebies and promotions
14. Look at sales and targets
15. Think about customer service
16. Make a map for customers to follow to make the most out of your products...

Analyse

Let's briefly evaluate what each area requires you to do.

Take a very large plain sheet of paper. Start from the centre.

To do	
1. We will capture your ideas,	Create a mind map/spider diagram. Get a sheet of paper and write down your business name. Draw a circle around it and draw out 20 spikes radiating from it. Try to answer these per spike. 1. What does your business do or provide? 2. Name 5 benefits it brings 3. Give3 limitations (Which it does not do) 4. What assets do you already have? 5. What assets do you need to have? 6. How much revenue do you need annually? 7. Do you have a FUTURE VISION written down now? 8. What are you own skills/Profile? 9. What Skills/profiles will you need to bring in? 10. Have you specific goals regarding actual sales? 11. Do you have a team now? 12. Do you have the relevant connections? 13. Do you have finance in place to cover 3 months? 14. Do you have experience in this field? 15. Do you need training for this? 16. Is there a pricing structure in place? 17. Who is your main competition? 18. What is your technical skill (out of 10)? 19. Add two other areas of you own choice.
2. Inspect the options	Look at the map you have just drawn. Take one Spike (e.g. What does your business provide?) and add a spike onto it and expand on this in a word or two. Add another spike from THAT as you go deeper into explaining it. Eventually you will have a mass of information. Take a look at the branch of spikes that has the most content for your business vision. Everything else can be postponed for now. Not forgotten. Just postponed.
3. Collect and categorise your assets	Collect and categorise all your current sellable assets on **Post-it notes** one by one including products and services. Give a brief one sentence description for each. Then give 3 benefits for a customer this would have and why. (Check out our **'Three Bucket Nugget'** Worksheet coming soon!)

	Do not skip this step.
4. Isolate your most likely Target Market	On another large sheet of paper add all your best customers' traits. Describe the following: 1. Gender: 2. Age range 3. Marriage status 4. Dependents 5. Location 6. Expendable income 7. Home owner 8. Medical condition 9. Hobbies 10. Pets 11. Education 12. Jobs 13. Emotional state 14. Other? 15. What is it they might need? 16. What social platform do they use the most? 17. (Add as many as you feel is relevant)
5. Map your best assets to your Target market	Take each **Post-it note** and place it on the best fit description of your ideal customer's traits. You now have a reason/ solution for your ideal customer and your product to be together. You can use this in your advertising and market strategies.
6. Check competition	Now we have an idea of your solutions and ideal customer, let's see who is doing something similar to you. If there is no one this is not always a great thing. It is harder to create and develop a whole new niche as it may be too small to be profitable. This may be why it does not yet exist. In a larger market you can evaluate what strategies others are using that work and you can then look inside your own business to isolate your own Unique Selling Point (USP). Find three similar companies to your own. Check out their turnover per annum. Is it high enough for your company to exist too?
7. Find your Unique Selling Point	Research what the competition is offering. Look at your own business and find that one thing that no one else seems to be providing that your target market would love to have. Is it unique to your company? If you have one, then you have just found your USP and this is the main reason why you can grow even when others

	compete with you. If they cannot duplicate your USP you are very very safe.
8. Set your price structure	With the USP comes the ability to charge a good price point and beat off competition. Most companies do not use their company brands anymore but their personal brand as this is linked to the individual, which should be you. Examine a price structure that still gives value to the client. When you have productised your assets, see if you can price them.
9. Get a timeline	By this time you have enough to plan your journey. All journeys should have a sensible timeline so that you can keep an eye on milestones and targets. You will be expected to learn about Benchmarking and Key Performance Indicators that will be hidden in your analytics (data from various sources like social media, web activity and sales). To illustrate a point here, making a million pounds is awesome, but not if you made it over a million years so you need to have a timeline and targets that work for your business. We have created a timeline for you to populate. Best method is to black out any time you spend on holidays and breaks and non-working non-negotiable time. Whatever else is left you can fill in with tasks. Planning is an art form with promotions and research and checkpoints so get help with this if you are unsure.
10. Brand yourself	Your individual attributes will be as Manna from Heaven to someone. Make sure you focus some time on developing a unique brand that will identify you in a room full of similar people. Your Brand could be your USP too. Look out for our **'Brand Yourself'** Worksheet coming soon.
11. Address Social media	Social media is your connection with the world. It is a Global platform so remember this when using. Use the media that your target market frequents the most. Get help with using social media if you are not proficient.
12. Check out joint ventures and partnerships	There are always opportunities with larger establishments that are already entrenched in your market place. They should not fear competition. In fact you can and should complement them. If you approach them with this viewpoint they will most likely allow you to share their database of existing hot leads. This can save you years of advertising and thousands of pounds.

13. Freebies and promotions	There are three basic types of clients or 'avatars'. They hardly ever morph into one another but believe they can. Understand that each have a very important value to your business and are not better than any other but are equal. The client that never wants to pay is your word of mouth mechanism. When they are happy then your business gets the best advertisement ever. They will be the largest volume to supply. They have time for you but not money. Make sure you provide value that you can afford to supply automatically, cost effectively and that you don't mind being spread all over. Give freebies, like online quizzes, PDF downloadable and Facebook groups which work well too. The client that has a small budget to spend also have their reasons why they will not breach their limit. It is up to you to put out feelers to find that point and package and productise your assets (which you have listed now in Post it notes) accordingly. Keep an eye on the monetary cost to you as well and make sure the value to the client far exceeds this. Books and webinars and workshops are ideal products. Here the client will add to the word of mouth mechanism and eventually reach… The higher paying client. These have the funds to invest if not the time. They are interested in your products which will make great return on investment but may be restricted as to available time in webinars or reading books unless they are extremely well set up. Create a high end package that provides a solution especially for them and indulge them in an experience that they cannot get elsewhere. They do like networking events so arrange it so they can book in like a weekend in a resort with you or a one to one session.
14. Sales and targets	Benchmarking is paramount if you want to track progress. Benchmarking is a target you set for a certain Key Performance Indicator. You can then divide this goal into Smaller steps. Just setting up milestones towards your ultimate target will help. (See **Benchmarks** Worksheet P.26) Begin with simple figures which have been 'SMART' aligned. (Specific Measureable, Achievable Realistic

	and timed P.44). First create your own end targets. Eg: £20,000 gross revenue to be made in 6 months from sales of hairclips. You now have the deadline: **6 months** The target: **£20,000 gross revenue** and you have specified what from The Product: **sales of hairclips.** Add this to you timeline and then pop in promotional plans accordingly. (Of around 3 months each).
15. Customer service	Consider how you will cater for this. You can outsource this now with many larger companies choosing to do so as well, you will not appear any different from them. This is an advantage.

Reference:

[https://www.entrepreneur.com/encyclopedia/target-marketSmall Business Encyclopedia 2016 www.entrepreneur.com]

Lastly, you will need a map of how your products fit together so your customer feels there is some thought and structure involved. It's very important to give them a structure of how you envision their journey. The downside of this is that they will buy into everything and not understand what they are doing after spending so much time and money and resentment can begin to creep in unless you are involved in their progress.

Suggest a journey for them even if they are paying or non-paying clients. People like to believe they CAN move into higher avatars. That's to be encouraged as clients should be made to feel appreciated. Suggest a route for the advancement from one type of client to another even though this is not guaranteed as it gives a real perspective to all and helps illuminate progress and results they can expect in each level. If they choose to move onwards that's super awesome. If they do not, then that's perfectly fine too.

Design

Ok so it's time to collect all your research and work.

Place your mind map/Spider diagram on a blank wall where you can see it. Add to it when you learn more.

Use The Three Bucket Nugget System to collect new ideas and add them to your mindmap as time goes by. You will see opportunities better this way and even focus on areas that are in need of products.

Add your target market next to the mindmap and see if you can refine and tweak this to isolate a single person that you can direct all your promotion and information to. Making things personal makes your client feel special as if you know them which make your business more attractive. Blog or tweet any special interest items or news stories that relate to them as weeks go by.

Look at prices per type of customer avatar. See where you can add more assets (value) yet keep your mark up. Make it clear to customers that you have added value to the tune of £x for free. Try not to overcrowd and confuse the products however.

Add your timeline to your wall as well. Colour code it if it helps. Make sure you keep as close as possible to it and check daily. Tick off as you go or make updates directly on it.

Mark your sales benchmarks on the timeline now if you haven't already.

Develop

Give yourself a month to set up and sort out the timelines and customer service outsourcing. Repeatedly analyse your To Do list to reflect your own business needs.

Test

Make sure you test each aspect of the To do list and tasks over time. It is important that you get real value from these Practical Worksheets.

For some it will provide an overnight success. For others it will require more time as each business will need to adapt and grow in order to provide a better fit for your target market which is different per business. Do not panic if you cannot complete all the parts first time! This is a process that you need to give great thought to if you are really looking for a structure that can move you forwards.

Unfortunately each person's path is different, however this format should provide enough of a sound pathway that will separate quite a lot of your requirements so you can isolate areas that need more work and development. That's fine. Businesses all grow and develop over time. Think of it as a garden that needs nurturing in order to get your bounty. Adapt any aspects you wish, to fit your business.

Evaluate

After a week stop and ask yourself if you now feel you have captured your business ideas, solidified, packaged and priced your assets in order for others to understand.

How does that make you feel?

What have I discovered?

1. I understand that my business ideas need to be captured, solidified, packaged and priced in order for others to understand.
2. I have captured, solidified, packaged and price my assets in my business now.

Thank you to Sonia Czernik for suggesting a Practical worksheet to capture visions and set out a plan of action for Entrepreneurs!

ORGANISATIONAL
RESCUE

Pricing.

(Daniel Priestley Suggestion)

Steel Energy Task
https://www.geniusu.com/my-genius-test

Objective:

1. To understand why I need a pricing sheet.
2. To create a basic pricing sheet, for my business.

Identify

Setting clear price structures is a very important factor that many entrepreneurs fail to do.

When pricing there are many aspects to take into consideration so we are only going to look at a few.

Firstly you should endeavour to be transparent. Clearly indicate the service or product as the cost to the buyer. List the attributes clearly (think of how Amazon sell) and then make it clear the price the buyer will ultimately pay.

Avoid hidden extra charges. Show all taxes clearly. This tends to give your business the reputation that is professional and not going to get one over on the customer. Transparency on price is your friend and will mean a higher chance of returning business.

Pricing can depend on scarcity, perceived value and actual cost to create. Have a think about payment methods if you are getting resistance to prices that you really cannot drop any lower. Subscriptions and memberships allow for spreading the cost however if you are paying out for costs consider how you will cover your costs at the very least if cancellations happen.

Tier your products and services to allow easier access for different people. Check out your competitors or if you have a Unique Selling Point (Your branding) you could charge on your own merits.

Think about either adding more value to your products on a regular basis over the year to keep it competitive instead of decreasing the price that is once the products sells, try not to decrease the price but instead increase the perceived value given, keeping your product competitive.

Make sure to highlight each monetary value to your client clearly.

Do not compete on price. Instead work on unique value. If a client bases their purchase solely on cost, then they are not the type of customer that will likely return anyway and will therefore not be as valuable to you but there will be others that are.

Try to add the information so it is located physically near to the price.

Analyse

1* The attributes of your product or service should get the attention of your target audience. This is not to say it is what the target audience needs but more what they WANT. A person that has fallen arches in their feet may NEED arch support in their shoes but WANT that sparkling shiny pair with no support and ultimately will end up buying that instead regardless of its disadvantages. We are not suggesting you are unethical at all but it is important to realise that if there is no interest for a need, such as a sole support then you sales will reflect this. People buy what they want, not what they need, no matter how much you spell this out. It is the way of the world.

2* If you are selling in your own country make sure you include all relevant taxes. If you sell abroad make sure you notify the correct revenue offices as to what countries citizen you are so you pay only the tax in your country. Some countries and states also have their own taxes so check this before adding it to the total price. You can break it down if you wish for transparency. Adding this afterwards is always a put off. Postage should be separate.

3* Payment methods can include monthly/weekly subscriptions which means the client has less of a large sum to pay up front. Freemium options give a free but restricted version where payments happen on further add on products. Fremiums are loss leaders as they are given away to generate more revenue later.

4* Making your products really easy to purchase makes a noticeable difference.

Are your buy buttons confusing? Are they trapped under page after page of text? Are they at the bottom of a looooong web page? Are they the same colour as the background so it's hard to see? Do you have a mass of confusing text?

5* Believe it or not, your company has a unique value that cannot be found elsewhere.

YOU.

Even if it means a little access to yourself, this can be a Unique Selling Point that adds to your sale. Things like access to a Facebook group or Instagram or other social media like blogs or newsletters that you give regularly or tweets you automate with your own unique motivational viewpoints or even free webinars you do already...

Design

It is now time to stop and apply your own particular answers. I strongly suggest taking your time to go over these in a neutral space where you would normally go to deep think without being disturbed.

QUESTIONS	ANSWERS
1* Find at least 4 'wants' (You can use feedback forms or questionnaires).	
Break down the cost of providing this.	
2* What are the taxes liable in your country?	
3* What payment methods can you offer on your product or service?	
4* Find 3 ways to Make your products more easy to purchase.	
5* Give 3 small things that add value to your product or service that can be duplicated free, yet give value...	

Develop

This is where you apply these to your business and watch what happens.

If you have Google analytics or other metric you can use to track your flow of customers to your webpage and your sales page I suggest you print screen the data before you change anything so you have a control to measure the results by.

Test

Take a few days and the return to your metrics and print screen it again. Compare the two results to see what affect the changes made had. It is important to understand the meaning of what you are looking at.

Look out for any negative results like drop off on sales or less time spent on a sales page or abandoned shopping carts. This is a negative Key Performance Indicator.

The beauty of this is that you can return and adjust your values again and again until your Key Performance Indicators give you better results.

Evaluate

What did you find? Consider if you would do anything different? What ideas has this given you to move forwards?

What have I discovered?

1. I understand why I need a pricing sheet.
2. I can create a basic pricing sheet, for my business.

- ***A massive thank you to Daniel Priestley co-founder and director of DENT Global and the Key person of Influence Brand accelerator for the suggestion!***

References:

http://www.acrwebsite.org/search/view-conference-proceedings.aspx?Id=7008

https://en.wikipedia.org/wiki/Freemium

http://summitevergreen.com/why-tiered-pricing-is-the-only-way-to-price-your-product/

ORGANISATIONAL
RESCUE

Hiring People

(Jon Masters suggestion)

Blaze Energy Task
https://www.geniusu.com/my-genius-test

Objective:

1. To sift through applicants to make a good decision with a ranking criteria
2. To create the basic ranking criteria for my vacancy.

Identify

A logical system of working through application forms in order to isolate the best fit for the position advertised.

There is a large amount of data that is provided in various forms both electronic and paper based that you may have gathered. Ideally collected in a format that is logical such as a database or spreadsheet.

You should have a list of criteria that you used when advertising.

In sorting a list of candidates there are various methods that can be used however we will be looking at upper and lower bounds sorting where the candidates are categorised and numerically assigned a value then they are clearly split into an upper and lower bound area.

Those that fall in the upper bounds are the candidates who are more likely to fit the role than the lower bound candidates.

This less exacting option allows for the human factor such as whether that person will fit the company vision, if that person leaves before start date for another job, if the applicant feels that position was not as expected, if other personal issues stop them from accepting the role.

You will at least have a fall back of a variety of candidates at the time for the role you advertised.

Spreadsheets are a great way of filtering data in this fashion.

Analyse

Here are a few things that you will need to allow yourself in carrying out this task:

- How many people do you have time to interview?

- How much time do you wish to devote to this? (Deadlines)
- What are the top 50% most relevant criteria to the position?
- What 2 aspects of each candidate clearly indicates to you that this person exhibits this skill/trait?
- Test result (If applicable) and pass mark. (25/30).
- Team Dynamic Profile? (In each team (regardless of professional role) requires a personality trait that is complementary to the team dynamic... Do you know the candidates)
- Candidate accepted: Salary or pay?
- Job role/duty?
- Hours of work?
- Your terms and conditions?
- Benefits?
- Holidays
- Expected dress code and behaviour,
- Supplied evidence for
- Qualifications
- experience (references),
- Specific competencies for the role.
- CV shows evidence of adaptability/Lifelong learning.
- CV is mostly consistent with current job direction.
- CV shows innovative capabilities
- CV has no large unexplained periods.
- Level of collaboration (works alone, in pairs, teams, mixture)

Design

How many people do you WANT to interview?	3
Team Dynamic Profile required.	MECHANIC
Score 1 for each answer	Yes also = 1 no = 0

	Candidate needs.															Candidate accepts.							
Name	[1 criteria relevant*] is possessed	[1 criteria relevant*] is possessed	[1 criteria relevant*] is possessed	[1 criteria relevant*] is possessed	[1 criteria relevant*] is possessed	[1 criteria relevant*] is possessed	Team Dynamic Profile of candidate is as required?	Qualification evidence given	Experience (references) checked ok	Has other specific competencies for the role.	Evidence of adaptability/Lifelong learning.	CV is mostly consistent with current job direction.	CV shows innovative capabilities	Other	Other	Candidate has accepted: Salary or pay?	Job role/duty accepted	Hours of work accepted	Your terms and conditions Accepted	Benefits understood	Holidays accepted	Expected dress code and behaviour accepted	TOTAL SCORE
Sue smith	1	1	1	1	1	1	1	1	1	1	1	1	1	1	1	1	1	1	1	1	1	1	22
James plum	1	1	1	1	1	1	1	1	1	1	1	1	1	1	1	1	1	1	1	1	1		21
Andy muray	1	1	1	1	1	1	1	1	1	1	1	1	1	1	1	1	1	1	1	1			20
Fred Astaire	1	1	1	1	1	1	1	1	1	1	1	1	1	1	1	1	1	1	1	1			20

You can create your own Spreadsheet and use a scoring system. (Actual Spreadsheet available from Organisational Rescue).

Develop

This consists of filling in the sheet above by working across each row and inserting a 1 for a positive answer.

Test

Use this to locate as many candidates for your position in the shortest time with the greatest accuracy. Adapt the data as you see fit.

Evaluate

After testing did you find this was a faster more effective way of selecting a set of suitable candidates for your vacancy?

What have I discovered?

1. I can now sift through applicants to make a good decision with a ranking criteria
2. I can now create the basic ranking criteria for my vacancy.

Thank you to Jon Masters Director at VISYONR and Eric Solot, MD of Alpha Power Solutions, who also requested this Practical Worksheet solution!

ORGANISATIONAL
RESCUE

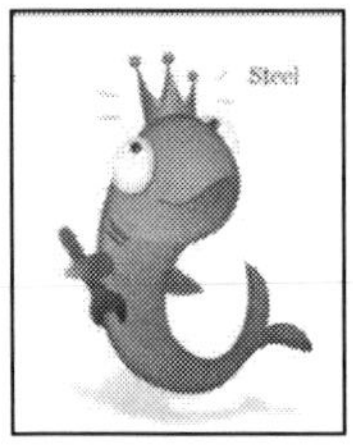

Forms

(Daniel Priestley Suggestion)

Steel Energy Task
https://www.geniusu.com/my-genius-test

Objective:

1. To understand why I need a sign up form.
2. To create a basic sign up form for my business.

Identify

We will be looking at electronic sign up forms

These are the authorisation forms you will require in order to start a contract or agreement with your client...

Your Sign up form should be as simple as possible to encourage speedy throughput and can be as simple as name and email details with a large submit button that actually explains what's happening next.

Make sure you give a real good but brief explanation of the reason to sign up. Most sign up forms will offer a barter exchange (known as a 'lead magnet') for the information of something valuable to and from the client/customer. Generally speaking it will be the clients personal details like email address. You can agree to provide a downloadable file or an online test or anything you wish.

These are used to capture the first level of interest from your target audience and do not guarantee that they will later exchange money for your products but it does allow you to build an email list. (There is beginning to be some debate about the usefulness of email lists due to the phenomenal load of emails now being distributed and usually not read. People also do not generally like to be chased up if they have not had time to read your awesome emails either...)

Also include a privacy policy of not sharing data and keeping it secure. (Data Protection Act 1998)

As long as the information is short concise and looks congruent with your webpage a good sign up form can hit up to 35% success rate.

Recent thoughts are 'Captchas' put people off so use the double opt-in email instead to deter robots spam.

Analyse

Let's analyse the reasons for of an online form:

The classic sales funnel consists of capturing customers through marketing then leading them onto sales to close the deal. Keep this in mind.

Online forms are linked to marketing programs that can store track and send out emails to subscribers automatically like Active campaigns,

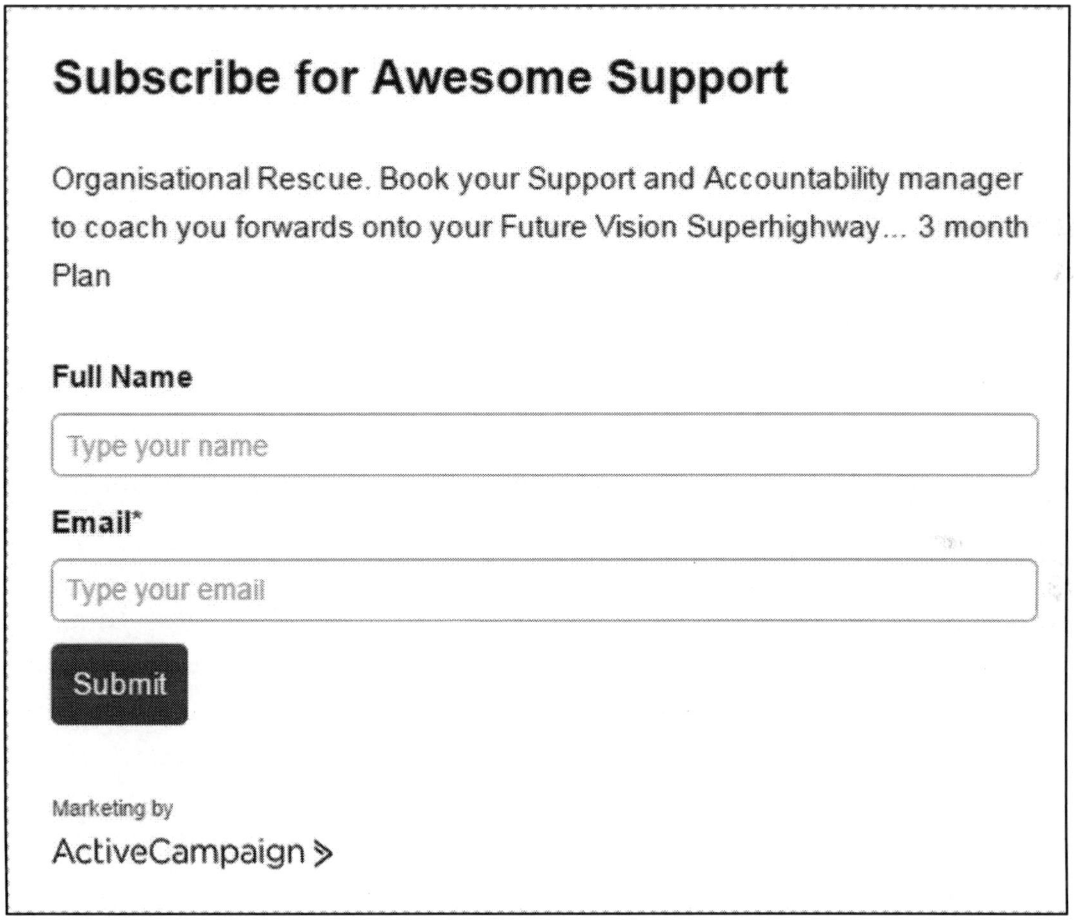

You can choose other marketing software like Hub spot, Ontraport and others.
http://www.capterra.com/marketing-automation-software/

Marketing software operates at the start of the sales funnel where you are beginning to get raw leads and nudging them slowly to marketing qualified leads where they are ready to spend with you.

After this point at the end of the sales funnel, you need to make sure you save the details of sales and what and when per person automatically so you can then use this to send other relevant products to them or further individualise your service by connecting at special times like birthdays.

Salesforce, Insightly and Zoho are an example of CRM's . If you want to have one program that does it all, then try Infusion soft or Hubspot. (We do not receive any affiliation payments for any of the suggestions made and other options exist).

The form is the beginning of the sales funnel that should lead to your sale. It is so important that you create a simple form with as little to deflect your audience as possible.

https://zapier.com/learn/ultimate-guide-to-crm-apps/marketing-automation-crm/

Design

In all truthfulness you should be able to create this on your chosen software in minutes. Select the right option to embed link or add to Facebook too. The design should be simple and link in with the corporate colours of your logo (3 main colours).

Develop

You can add Captchas if you wish to change the format or if you are getting spam bot coming through. Make sure you have a double opting-in subscription which covers you if the customer doesn't remember ever having filled in your form. If they opt in again then your system will keep the data and they cannot accuse you of SPAM...

Test

Create two very distinct forms for the same product and test these out for a week. Make sure you can use analytic to trace the footfall usage of each version, whichever one is outperforming the other will let you change and perfect parts of the form.

Evaluate

After a week testing out two forms what did you observe as a positive result?

What have I discovered?

1. I understand why I need a sign up form now.
2. I can create a basic sign up form for my business.

- ***A massive thank you to Daniel Priestley co-founder and director of DENT Global and the Key person of Influence Brand accelerator for the suggestion!***

ORGANISATIONAL

RESCUE

Decision Engine

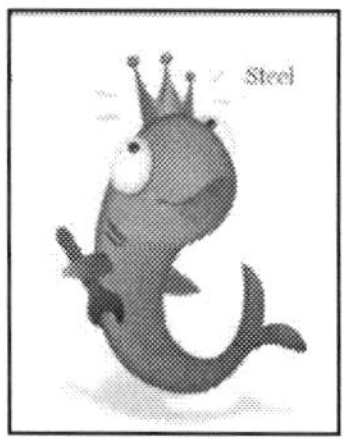

Steel Energy Task
https://www.geniusu.com/my-genius-test

(Julian Farquhar suggestion)

Objective:

1. To sift through criteria to make a good decision via a ranking criterion
2. To create a basic ranking criteria for my own decisions.

Identify

There are many types of decision making options out there, most of which involve a complicated flowchart.

If you are looking for a logical system of working through decisions in order to isolate the best outcome for a problem there will usually be many variables to consider, many outcomes possible and many branches from A to B. Flowcharts can get messy and have to be updated for each possible candidate and comparing them is not simple.

The scenario is: You will have a list of criterion or rules that you wish to fit.

You will also have a number of options or candidates that are to be considered quickly against these that you can immediately visually compare.

You want a way that you can simply play with the variables and not have to wait for complicated mathematical analysis to conjure up a best fit.

Spreadsheets are a great way of manipulating data in this fashion.

- Note: This decision Engine is a version of the Hiring People Engine created for Jon Masters earlier. What this illustrates, I hope, is that spreadsheets are a versatile solution that can be put to many uses. Indeed the Flow or Outsource Engine also is based on a similar solution.

Analyse

Let's assume it's a decision for business to take on more staff and you have to objectively come to a practical solution.

Here are a few things that you will need to allow yourself in carrying out this task:

What are the top 10 criteria to fit to as yes no questions?

Eg:

1. 1 Relevant criteria is possessed
2. 1 Relevant criteria is possessed
3. 1 Relevant criteria is possessed
4. 1 Relevant criteria is possessed
5. 1 Relevant criteria is possessed
6. Team Dynamic Profile (In each team a personality trait that is complementary to the team dynamic)
7. Qualification evidence given
8. Experience checked
9. Other specific competencies
10. Evidence of adaptability and lifelong learning
11. CV mostly consistent with current job direction
12. CV shows innovative capabilities
13. Other
14. Other
15. Candidates accept: salary/pay
16. Job role/duty accepted
17. Hours of work accepted
18. Your terms and conditions accepted
19. Benefits understood
20. Holidays accepted
21. Expected dress code and behaviour accepted

These are just an idea of the criteria you might have in mind that describes the prefect outcome.

The same format holds true for any decision.

If you can identify outcomes as a positive (YES) list them in this way now.

1	
2	
3	
4	
5	
6	
7	
8	
9	
10	
11	
12	
13	
14	
15	
16	
17	
18	
19	
20	
21	
22	

Design

You can create your own Spreadsheet with the above and use a scoring system. You can get a copy from the Organisational Rescue Website and fill in as required with your own specific criteria.

Just replace the values across the top of the sheet with your own!

Add the names of the candidates to evaluate.

Across each now add a '1' in every cell across the sheet where the person has scored a 'YES'.

The decision engine will immediately calculate a **total score** for you.

In fact you can already see quite easily exactly which candidate is the best fit according to the criterion you've set as this method is very transparent.

I use this to work with over 500 student's progression and I can easily filter off the top scorers and pick up ones that need help so it's been invaluable for sorting through massive amounts of data in an instant.

How many people do you WANT to interview?	3	Score 1 for each answer
Team Dynamic Profile required.	[illegible]	Yes also = 1 no = 0

Candidate needs / Candidate accepts

Name	1. Does this person hold the X qualification required?	2. Does this person have more than [3] years in the field?	3. Are their references ok?	4. Has the person worked in a team?	5. Has the persons worked alone?	6. Are there no gaps in their CV history?	7. Are they in the right price bracket?	8. Are they immediately available?	9. Have they worked on a imilar project before?	10. Do they have a network of similar pport they can call on?	11. Team Dynamic Profile?	12. Candidate accepted: Salary or pay?	13. Job role/duty accepted?	14. Hours of work accepted?	15. Your terms and conditions accepted?	16. Benefits accepted?	17. Holidays or period of non-work accepted	18. Expected dress code d behaviour accepted.	19. Additional and ecific competencies for	20. CV shows evidence of adaptability/Lifelong learning.	21. CV is mostly onsistent with current job direction.	22. CV shows innovative capabilities	TOTAL SCORE
Sue smith	1	1	1	1	1	1	1	1	1	1	1	1	1	1	1	1	1	1	1	1	1	1	22
James plum	1	1	1	1	1	1	1	1	1	1	1	1	1	1	1	1	1	1	1	1	1		21
Andy muray	1	1	1	1	1	1	1	1	1	1	1	1	1	1	1	1	1	1	1	1			20
Fred Astaire	1	1	1	1	1	1	1	1	1	1	1	1	1	1	1	1	1	1	1	1			20
	1	1	1	1	1	1	1	1	1	1	1	1	1	1	1	1	1	1	1	1			20
	1	1	1	1	1	1	1	1	1	1	1	1	1	1	1	1	1	1	1				19

Develop

This consists of you carrying out the task and filling in the sheet above!

Test

Use this to locate as many practical solutions for your problem in the shortest time with the greatest accuracy. Adapt the data as you see fit.

Evaluate

Did you find this was a faster more effective way of selecting a set of suitable solution for your decision? Did you come to a suitable decision faster and are you more satisfied with the result?

What have I discovered?

1. I can now sift through criteria to make a good decision via a ranking criterion
2. I now have basic ranking criterion to help my decisions.

- ***Thank you to Julian Farquhar Creative Director and Business Partner at Jobcafe, for the awesome suggestion for our Practical Worksheets!***

ORGANISATIONAL
RESCUE

Dynamo Energy Task
https://www.geniusu.com/my-genius-test

Brochures

(Daniel Priestley Suggestion)

Objective:

1. To understand why I need a brochure for my core product and service and what goes into one.
2. To create a basic plan for a brochure and a chance to create it.

Identify

In today's age of electronic information, websites and blogs it's hardly surprising that people don't think about creating a brochure of their product and services but this is truly a missed opportunity according to Entrepreneur expert, Daniel Priestley.

Having a hard copy of your product adds credibility to a company giving the appearance of a longer lasting more stable business. Adding telephone numbers and lots of other contact details also assures the client or customer that you are not a one night stand or fly by night establishment ready to disappear with their money, or be impossible to contact right after a sale is made.

One should be as open and transparent as possible to assure people that you are there to help them and see that their pain points are fixed, not your own. This encourages return of customers which is much more cost effective than try to win new ones.

Even if you plan to outsource this, you should have a good idea of what you would like to final brochure to look like. Let's investigate that now.

Analyse

As we said, you may well outsource your brochure creation and we advise that you do, but it is still important that you are clear about the message your business is giving so you can be consistent in your message.

So what goes into your brochure?

Logo Colour

The logo is your 'badge' and will conjure up specific feelings in your target market.

Colours, shapes, font styles and emphasis have a psychological meaning to the person viewing it so you should have control of what that should be.

Here's a practical task:

Look up 'Darth Vader' on the internet. You should get a figure that is quite imposing and intimidating. Think of 3 words this image makes you feel...

Colours without being consciously aware, the selection and shade you choose will be very influential.

Now Search for PINK DARTH VADER.

Tell me you didn't smile. You smiled right?

Ok so we have established the power of colours. Enough said.

1. **THINK: write down 3 'feelings' you want your company to emit first.**
2. **Locate the 3 colours that match those feelings.**
3. **Write them down here:**

FEELINGS	COLOURS

Logo Shape

Let's look at shapes and their effects on people.

There are various interpretations but the simplest one to keep in mind is the instinctive feeling associated with hard masculine and soft feminine shapes called the Bouba Kiki effect. When one is asked to draw an abstraction of a sound that is abrupt, shrill and piercing like KIKI what shape would you draw? How about drawing a shape that matches the smooth fluid and soft sound of BOUBA?

Each of these has a definite associated feeling that comes across and this is fundamental in creating a logo that is congruent with your identity as a business. If you were a business dealing with meditation and wellbeing would you create a Bouba or a Kiki shaped logo?

If you were a business dealing with jet skis would you create a Kiki or Bouba shape? Or indeed a mixture?

All important things to keep in mind.

1. **THINK: write down the 3 'action' that you want your company to emit.**
2. **Create 'Bouba' or 'Kiki' shapes that match those feelings.**
3. **Draw them here.**

ACTION DESCRIPTION	BOUBA OR KIKI SHAPES

USP

Your 'Unique Selling Point' should be one of the prominent aspects of your marketing and branding. In a business world that is increasingly vying for attention from every conceivable angle, having something that speaks to your specific target market that is uniquely your strengths that they can have for a price. That means that without you even trying, **you are what you are selling**. It will not matter than someone else tries to copy you. They will never be YOU. At best they will always be an imitation. That's still second. Simply because you are and will always be the ultimate definition of your Unique Selling Point and THE solution to their pain.

1. **THINK: write down 4 unique things about you (Jobs, Training, Life experience, etc.).**
2. **Write a sentence that includes these to create your 'Unique Selling Point'.**

STRENGTHS	USP

Products

Depending on the type of brochure (electronic or hard copy or both, large or small) your products should be clear and visible. Grab Attention, boost their Interest and increase their Desire to own the product then call them to Action. This is **AIDA**. Be concise and brief.

1. **What would grab your target audience's attention?**
2. **What would boost their interest?**
3. **What would increase the desire to own your product?**
4. **What is your call to action?**

ATTENTION?	
INTEREST?	
DESIRE?	
CALL TO ACTION?	

Company vision or message

Headlines get at most a 3 second glance and need to capture the benefit the person wants and pull them into the solution you are providing. Make sure your slogan or tag line is short and to the point maybe 3 words long. Find images or text, which makes an impact with your background or corporate colours. Add a testimonial from a genuinely happy customer. Stress the benefits.

1. **What is your slogan or tag line? (3 words eg: 'Just do it')**
2. **Name 5 images* that would make an impact on your brochure (*Depends on size of brochure)**
3. **What colours would stand out from your own 3 colours picked at the beginning?**
4. **Find one awesome testimonial from a customer.**

SLOGAN OR TAG LINE	
NAME 5 IMAGES	
3 COLOURS THAT WOULD STAND OUT	
ONE AWESOME TESTIMONIAL	

Compelling angle& Call to action

Have you ever watched a four year old in a sweet shop? How long do they look at any one thing? What is their deciding pain point? What catches their eye? What makes them take grab one product over another? What's the negative pain if they wait? You have worked hard at grabbing their attention, they have decided to buy, -but oh look! A butterfly! They're off... All wasted. What limiting factor do they have to beat to get your awesome product? **If there is no scarcity, you could lose the sale**. If they feel they have beaten others to the prize they will value your product more.

1. **What are your target audience's pain points?**
2. **What's the negative for them if they delay buying? (Create one!).**

PAIN POINTS?	
NEGATIVE LIMITING FACTOR	

Design

You have in fact already completed the design ideas already above. Now create a plan using these ideas to create a first drawn-draft plan. (You can make the logo here or hire done on https://www.fiverr.com/too!)

You can get help creating a logo here:
http://logotypemaker.com/logo-maker

Here are a few samples that took 2 minutes online...

http://www.makelogoonlinefree.com/logomaker/
Here are a few more instant logos...

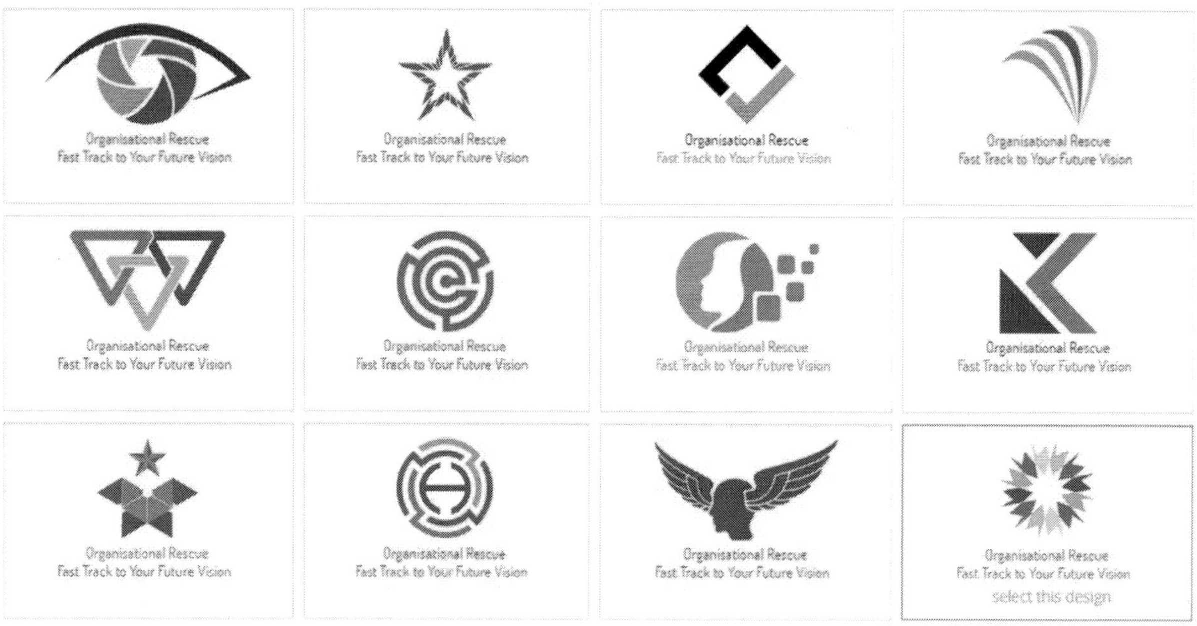

Here is an online brochure to get some ideas about layout and style... http://herbalifeproductbrochure.com/uk/brochure.shtml

Make your brochure downloadable as a PDF file like Jaguar does... http://www.jaguar.co.uk/request-a-brochure/index.html

Develop

You are now ready to create your brochure. You can choose to do it yourself using sources like these...

http://www.thegridsystem.org/free-brochure-templates/

http://www.stocklayouts.com/Templates/Free-Templates/Free-Brochure-Templates-Download.aspx

http://www.designvast.com/best-professional-brochure-templates-free-download/

http://www.formsbirds.com/free-marketing-brochure-template-5

Or get professionals to do it for you. Here are some companies that will create brochures for you.

http://www.vistaprint.co.uk/

https://www.instantprint.co.uk/

Test

Get a proof copy of one brochure and show it to two friends. Get feedback. Do not explain anything at all. Ask them what they understand just from the brochure itself about your business and product/service. This feedback will help you to perfect the brochure again and again. Repeat 3 times and then you will have a good version.

Evaluate

How did you find this process? Was it useful breaking down the section into smaller mini tasks and walking through them? How would you improve this method of creating brochures?

What have I discovered?

1. I now understand why I need a brochure for my core product and service and what goes into one.
2. I have created a basic plan for a brochure and had a chance to create it.

- ***A massive thank you to Daniel Priestley co-founder and director of DENT Global and the Key person of Influence Brand accelerator for the suggestion!***

ORGANISATIONAL

RESCUE

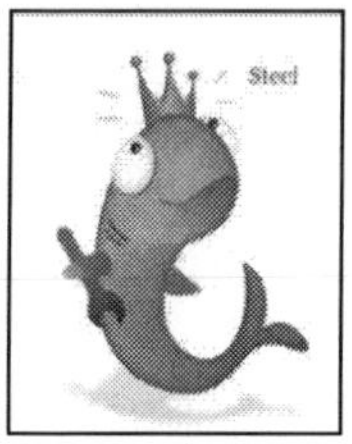

Processing Issues (Patrick Bet David suggestion)

Objective:

1. To understand that Processing Issues to find solutions in business is a key fundamental entrepreneurial skill.
2. To use a method to reliably break down a problem I have to find a solution.

Identify

What is the one thing that entrepreneurs should have to succeed in business?

Patrick Bet David feels very passionately about developing skills that solve processing issues.

He feels it is a fundamental core skill that can be applied to unravel all others.

So, what does 'Processing Issues' mean?

Well we can derive an answer as: "A series of operations in order to solve an important problem".

So what possible operations could this mean when facing a problem?

When problem solving many people use the 5 W's: What, when, where, who, why. (Even How if you like).

When a problem arises, you can use these questions to decompose it into its parts and examine each until it lays bare its secrets. Then by having an existing criterion by which you define success, you can match the best fit to it.

The problem is in the breaking apart and answering of the problem in the first place. Your decomposition of a problem may well be very different from someone else's and so it's better to have as many different mind-sets that understand your world and the solution in order to narrow down the options and fine stream the decomposition.

But first, let's set the SMART goal with a trip to the seaside.

Analyse

1) A desired outcome identified.

How do you know when you have arrived at a destination? You can identify it right? Not always.

Goals can be identified with a mind map if you are finding it hard to isolate what you want to achieve...

Here is a great tool –Freemind- (Many others exist) to create and map. http://freemind.sourceforge.net/wiki/index.php/Main_Page

Here is a first draft mind map of the problem. This helps get a feel for the problem.

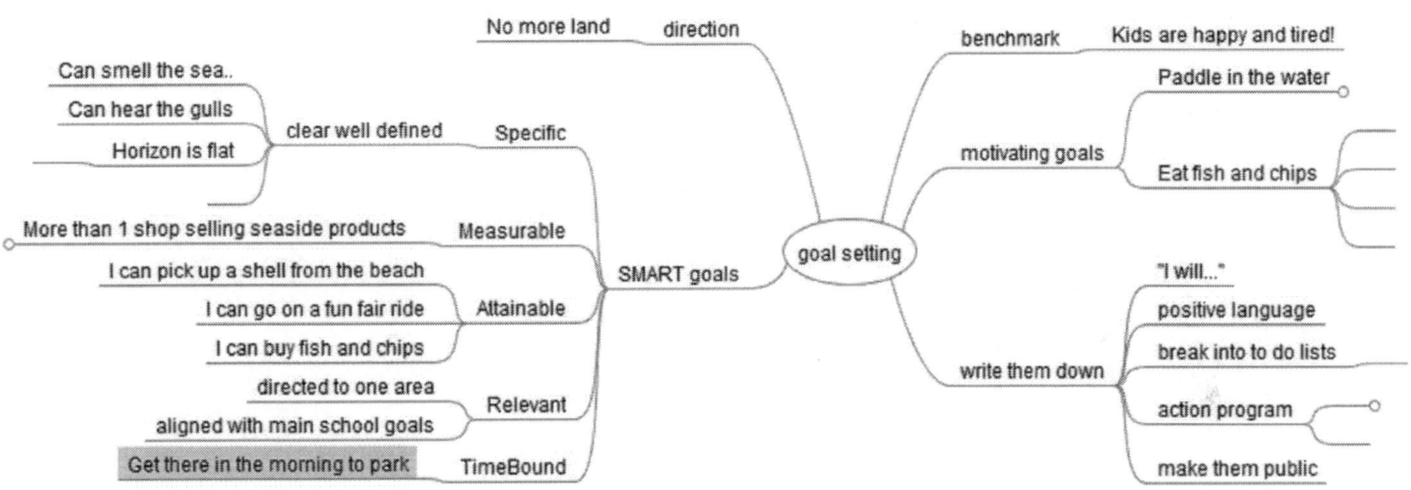

Destination	
Attributes	Met? (Y/N)
Smell of the sea	
Sound of the gulls	
Eat fish and chips	
Kids happy and tired	
Home by 7pm	

If you want to **go to the seaside with your kids for the day, eat fish and chips and go on the rides and be home by 7pm**, (SMART goals p.44).

Of course, a deeper breakdown would be required for deeper processing.

The issue

So returning to our question: WHERE DO I BEGIN?

Let's check the problem by examining the mind map and then take closer look...

Now although this is a simple example and I have not delved deeper into each area for the sake of clarity but what you should be able to see now is how the deeper reasons under each branch are coming forwards so can be addressed. Each can be expanded and detailed so that where your son, Fred might not be able to go on the rides, by bringing a nephew or niece along that can, your daughter can ride with them while you stay with your son watching. You can even plan which day to go and the best place to get a parking space. You can decide if you want to go to the fish and chips shop before or after the rides or bring sandwiches and drinks and just buy chips to share, to keep the cost down. It's all visible as it's all been processed.

Expecting the brain to solve all these issues on the go, is a tall order but by processing the issues visually in mind maps you can now easily isolate a solution that best fits your goal with comparative ease.

2. *The solution.*

You can now write a solution that fits closely with your original goal and be confident that the issue has been thoroughly processed.

"I will take my niece (who will sleep over) with my two kids and partner to Southend starting out at 7.00am, in my car on a Sunday and bring sandwiches and drinks that we can eat after the fun fair rides and share a bag of chips as we make sandcastles and return before 6pm".

Design

Ok Time to make it work for you:

Decide the issue that needs to be processed. It can be a goal, or something that identifies your end destination.

1) Fill in the spaces with descriptions of what the end goal will look like.

2) Now take the end attributes that best indicate your desired end goal from the mind map below and put them the table.

The end point has been now been processed.

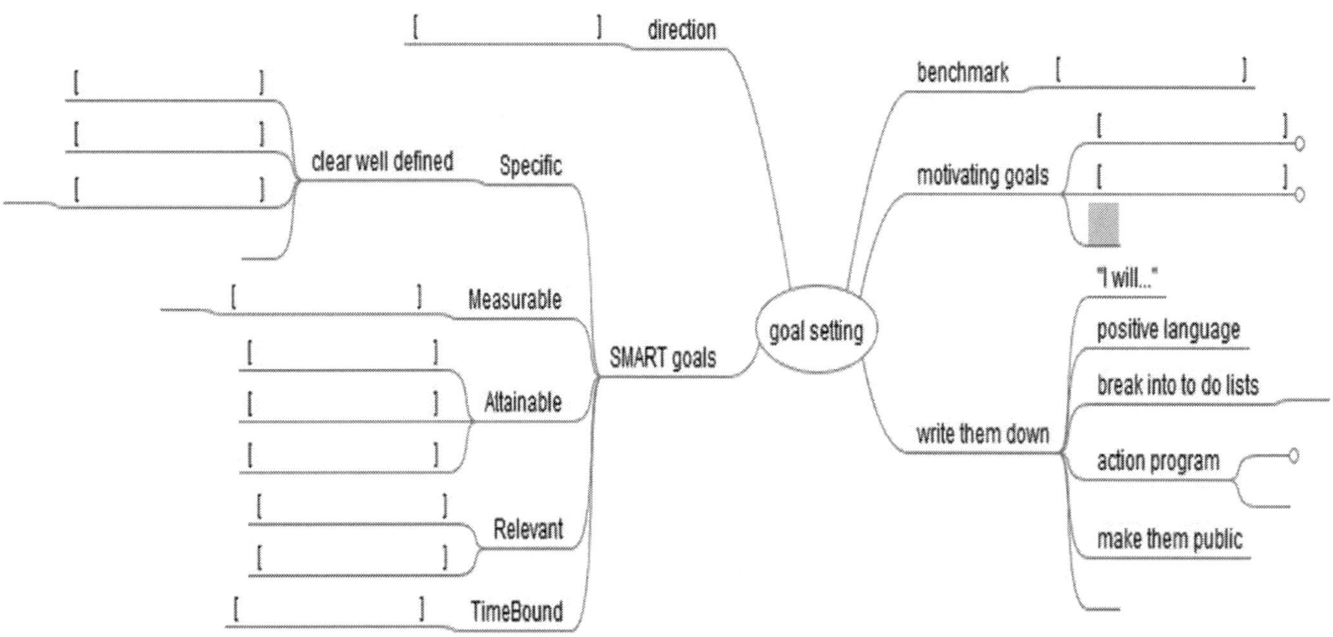

DESTINATION	
ATTRIBUTES	MET? (Y/N)

Take some time over this. Go to the coffee shop or somewhere you will not be disturbed.

(Note: There could be an infinite number of branches for any given section so you can only ever fill in the mind map with what you know at the current moment in time. For example if you filled this in next week you could come up with a totally different map. This is normal.)

3) Process the Issue deeper now. Break down as much of the problem as you possibly can. Make sure it has logical branches.

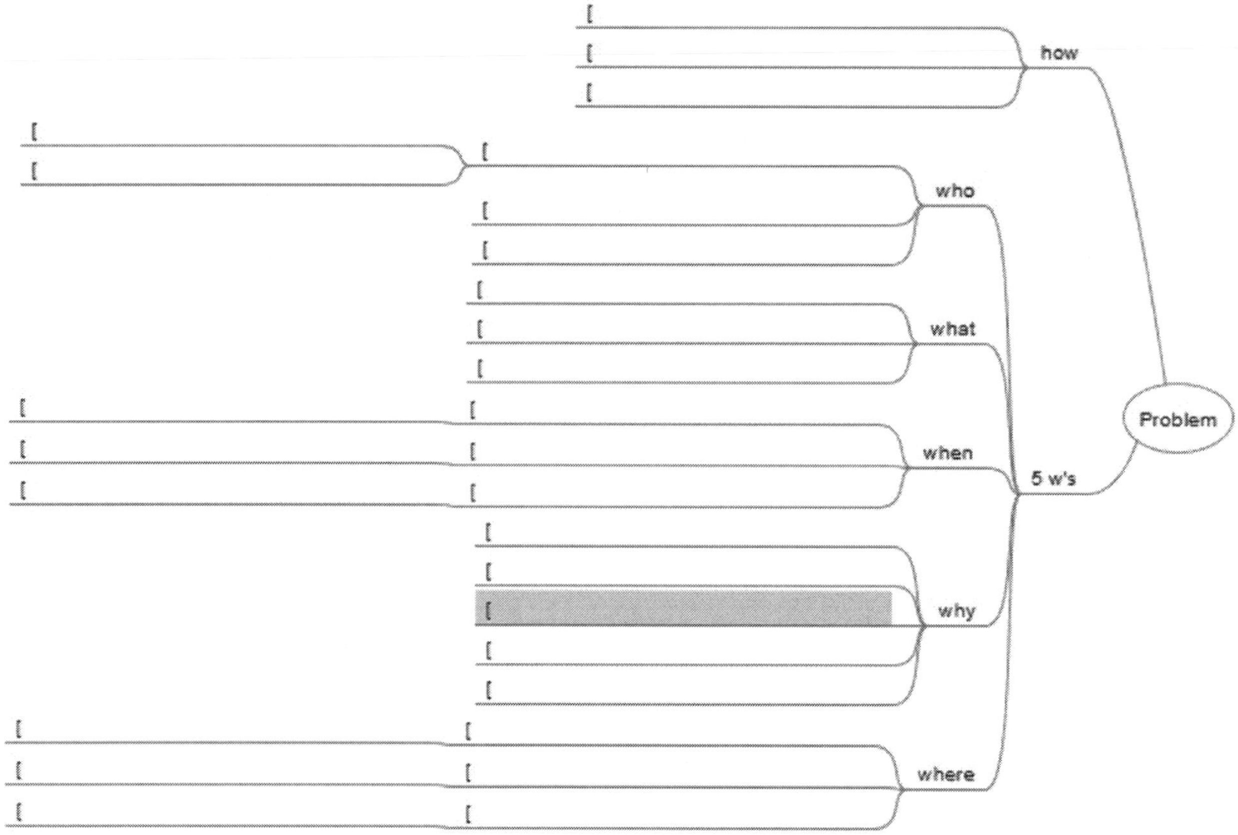

Don't feel you have to stop at the depth of the branches given. Extend or reduce as you see fit.

3) Now look at the end attributes from your table and see how this can be achieved FOR YOU AT THIS CURRENT MOMENT IN TIME with the processed issue above. If you need to extend the map more in certain areas do so. This is also normal. Processing is a very personal point of view.

You can now write a solution that fits closely with your original goal using what you have processed about the issue and be confident that the best solution has been captured with the current knowledge you have available.

Write it here: Here's a starting point you can use if you are having difficulties...

"I will ....and ...... and .... that I can ...."

Test

Take the solution that you have processed and use it. The only way you are going to find out if it works is to road test it. Check it does match all the attributes you processed out.

Evaluate

After a week return to the mind map and see if there is a better version you can create. Returning to process is always a good idea.

What alternative solutions to processing can you think of?

What have I discovered?

1. I understand that Processing Issues to find solutions in business is a key fundamental entrepreneurial skill.
2. I have used a method to reliably break down a problem I have and found a solution.

Thank you to Patrick Bet David for providing the problem for our Practical Worksheet solutions!

ORGANISATIONAL
RESCUE

Payment Issues

(Pascale J Petit suggestion)

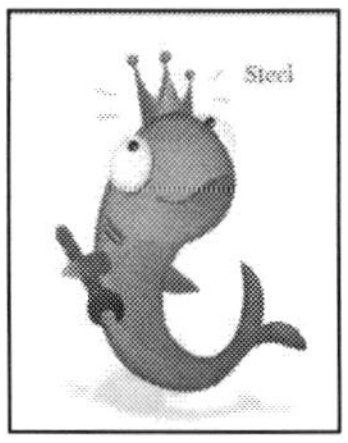

Steel Energy Task
https://www.geniusu.com/my-genius-test

Objective:

1. To understand the many various ways to receive payment by a client to prevent not being paid at all.
2. To create my own preferred method of payment that works for my business and me.

Identify

Working for yourself, demands a level of acumen around the risks of not being paid by clients.

Do not be convinced that a contract will definitely mean payment. Even having great Terms and Conditions could still mean that ultimately a non-paying client will turn out to be more costly in the end.

Let's take it from the viewpoint that your customer doesn't want to rip you off. From my own experience, most people are genuine in their desire to purchase and do value your goods so there has to be something else right? (There will also be others but we shall assume that the percentages of those are small and we shall look at how to make these smaller still).

Clients may want things for free. Some might have a genuine budget they cannot exceed. They may have a certain expectation on your service, product or solution. Your pricing strategy might not optimise for your product return on value, quantity of sales, or competition. Even your customer service may leave them in a panic and therefore affect the payment closure.

As we said, ultimately there may be some that will fall foul whatever you do so you can reduce these too.

Analyse

We can break these apart like so:

Clients that want freebies.

- There are people in the world that will never want to pay for your service and expect it for free. In the good old bad old days you put an ad in a magazine or Telly or radio and waited. You paid thousands and some turned up to buy. Now you have totally free advertising called SOCIAL MEDIA. Now to me, everyone that comes to you needs some level of help. You are not obliged to give them anything but what do you think people will say about your company if you actually give free help to those that really could use it? We've all been there in need, right? Ok no one will complain if you politely mention that there is a limit to how much freebies you can provide. We all have to make a living right? We all have bills to pay. We all have obligations. So, cap your freebies but make sure they are simple to use one off things that will cost you next to nothing and can be replicated for free. Think of this as your advertising budget. Make sure they are things that you would be happy to have spread around. This is your 'Fairy Dust'. Magic happens. Slowly, but it happens. Sprinkle liberally. Relieve the load of others. It's genuinely a nice feeling and people will talk about it positively (hopefully) and it won't have cost you a thing. Create You Tube clips, downloadable pdfs or online quizzes... [Use: Company Branding]

Clients with a budget.

- There are people in the world that will pay but a limited amount for a limited time or once. It is your task to package up a sensible offer and price it so that it is giving great value to the buyer yet is cost effective for you to produce. In the past this was bulk purchasing. Now it's more group exposure and support with a community feeling. This tends to provide a nice space for your specific niche and give your business that Unique Selling Point. Without this you are back to competing on price and this is a losing war when competing with others globally. There is only one you. If people want to be associated with you your personal branding will attract those and they will want to stay with you and be happy to have something associated with you. Create a low cost solution like a book or a webinar or a one off workshop. Payment up front. Some like month membership agreements and releasing products monthly. See how this would work for you but always release AFTER payment and stop automated release when payment fails. (https://www.infusionsoft.com/ and https://ontraport.com/). You can also suggest payment schemes for them if you see fit where you get paid the full sum and they pay the financer over a period. This is a payment method that reduces your risk. [Use: Verification of Affordability]

Clients that will pay more, happily.

- In any given group there are those that can and will pay more for that more exclusive product or service. They will be less in number however that number will never be zero. Everyone deserves to have a bit of you. Think of it that way. They can get a larger package that is more exclusive and gives a higher return on value. That's the way it goes. These people will have different requirements as they may have bigger deadlines and bigger demands on themselves too. They can still spend time with you or do the things needed with the product and by knowing the differences in your product you should be able to build up a really awesome package here. Add some other packages as well which you release for a limited time only. This encourages faster purchases. Follow a promotional plan around a 3 month strategy that uses the freebies, then the budgeted products then the high end stuff at the end. Always try to create urgency. These clients can afford upfront payments. You might offer a two part payment plan where the first part pays for all your costs so at least you get this before releasing your full load. Or split up the product into two parts and make sure payment is made beforehand (Pro forma). [Use: High end ROI]

'Love it, but do it for me' Clients.

- Again, don't get upset. There are genuinely people that literally love your stuff but don't have the time. Here's where you build a customised package around them.

  Make sure the price reflects your time as here is where you will spend most of it. As you can see, the lower end of your pricing strategy will mean less use of your time but the more costly means more of your time customising will be required and you should be compensated for that. Again upfront payments here are not unusual. [Use: Customisation and exclusivity].

All these people exist. You may not have had much experience of each level but they are there and they want your stuff.

It's your job to distinguish each person as they come to you. Why? Because good word of mouth is more valuable to you than 1000's on advertising and so each have a value to you as well as you having a value to them.

*** Remember: Don't expect a zebra to become an apple tree. One type of person rarely becomes another. It does happen but not as often as you**

might like. If you remember that each type of person possesses its own attributes and positives for your business, then you can then focus your energies profitably reducing the chance of not getting paid.

If you are finding a client is failing to pay you after a certain specified time, you can offer a solution of a financing company they can use to spread the cost over a longer term than you can provide and for a very reasonable cost. This may leave them happier as you have provided a positive solution for both of you. You get paid the remaining balance and you may even negotiate a reduction if they pay up quickly JUST THIS ONCE as they are clearly having difficulties. There are even companies that will buy your debt from you at a reduced value and then chase the client themselves. These are called Collection Agencies so you can get something back to cover your costs at least. Always provide written warning of impending action and stick to the dates. Alternatively you could add a small percentage for outstanding balance for each day it is overdue until it is resolved. You may also warn of court action for failure to pay.

Design

Let's break down your clients here:

TYPE	*Name*	*Value to my company (Company Branding/affordability/ High end ROI/Customisation)*	*Well-paying clients? (Y/N)*
Clients that want freebies.			(N/A)
Clients with a budget.			
Clients that will pay more, happily			
'Love it, but do it for me' Clients.			

Develop

Find out your perfect combination of clients by checking the cash flow from each possible source and matching against your monthly targets.

If you are experiencing an imbalance you will see it now. Take action to address that imbalance by creating more focus and products for the people you wish to attract. It is important that you realise where your best value is coming from and to think about the time you have and the price you charge so you can still be great value to your client but also maximise your intake and curb the time spent on areas that do not generate well-paying clients.

Test

Try this out for a month to check your results.

Did you find any hidden positives in the exercise? How will you use them? Do you think that you can identify and decrease your more challenging clients that do not pay? Which type of payment method works best for your business and clients?

What can you change to improve?

Evaluate

Do you feel that you have some better options for your clients to pay and increase the level of completed payments overall? Why?

What have I discovered?

1. To understand the many various ways to receive payment by a client to prevent not being paid at all.
2. To create my own preferred method of payment that works for my business and me.

*** Thank you to Pascale J Petit for providing the problem for our Practical Worksheet solutions!**

ORGANISATIONAL
RESCUE

To Flow or Outsource? (Christian Rodwell Suggestion)

Blaze Energy Task
https://www.geniusu.com/my-genius-test
© Wealth Dynamics
Replicated by kind permission of Roger James Hamilton

Objective:

1. To identify the characteristics of tasks in your business according to its attributes.
2. To identify exactly what tasks in my business are best for me to outsource or best for me to do myself.

Identify

"To flow or not to flow, that is the question".

As an entrepreneur there are times when you find yourself taking more and more tasks on and start to become unclear as to what could be better executed by others with a stronger affinity for the task.

The first sign of this may be when you realise your time is tight and your main focus is being diluted with things that take you out of your natural flow and feel like hard work.

Anything from, Designing a logo, video editing, social media posting, invoicing, marketing, networking or event planning to name a few all have very different energies that can either enrich your internal flow or zap it dead. Shouldn't you know which is which?

When you want a clear view of your business tasks and the areas you should be realigning to and those that you should outsource while on a tight budget you should begin by analysing all your various tasks attributes.

Let's do that now...

Analyse

As we mentioned these examples, let's look at a type of profiling that we can use to sort people.

We will use Roger James Hamilton's Wealth Dynamics profiling system to categorise types of people and skillsets that they may exhibit generally. (There are many people that overlap in skill sets. To understand your profile go to https://www.geniusu.com/ for the online profile test.

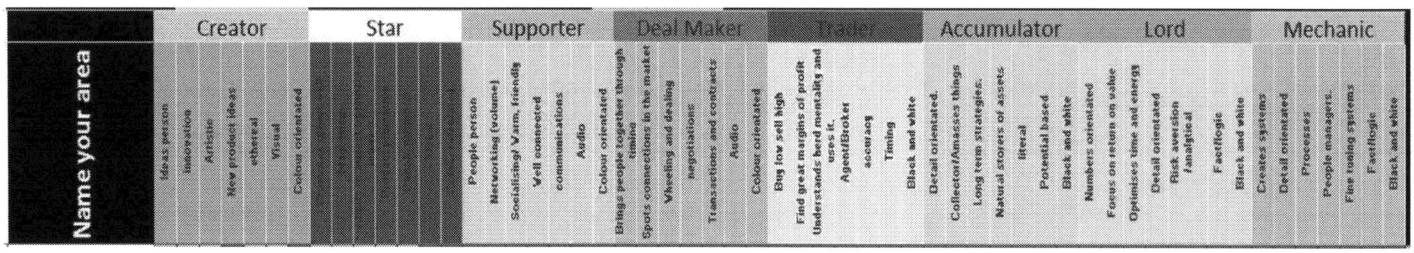

Under each profile we have isolated what we feel is a good trait of that profile. This does not change. DO NOT CHANGE THIS!

Here is a list of the tasks that you will need to sort. THIS YOU CAN UPDATE TO INCLUDE YOUR OWN TASKS (YES! REPLACE AS REQUIRED).

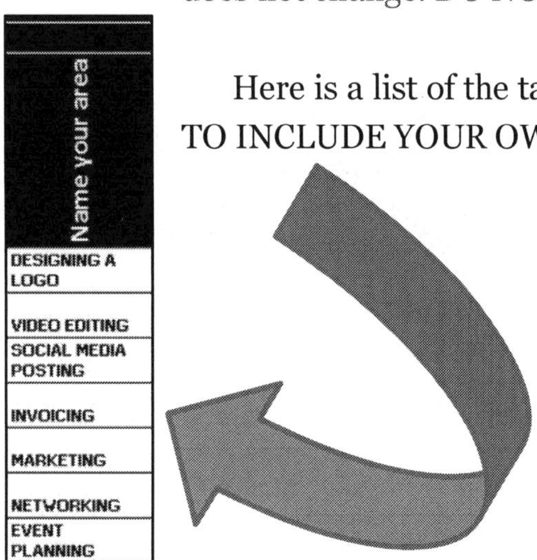

http://www.wealthdynamics.com/wealth-profiles/

Use this link to find out YOU OWN PROFILE.

Update the Flow or Outsource Engine with your profile. It will look something like this:

Here the user has set their profile as 'CREATOR'.

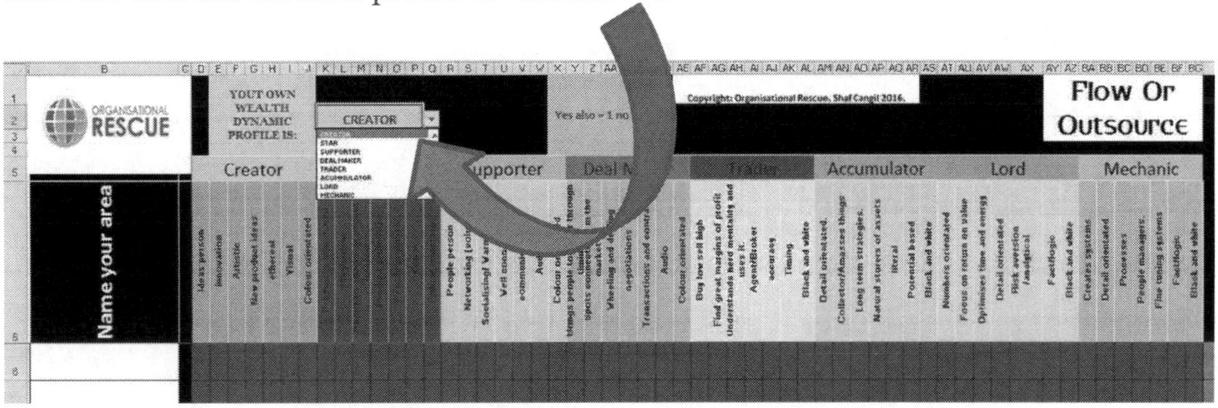

Now the work begins in earnest.

Go through the tasks **in a horizontal line** putting the number 1 into any red cell (box) that describes the task skills involved from the list above...

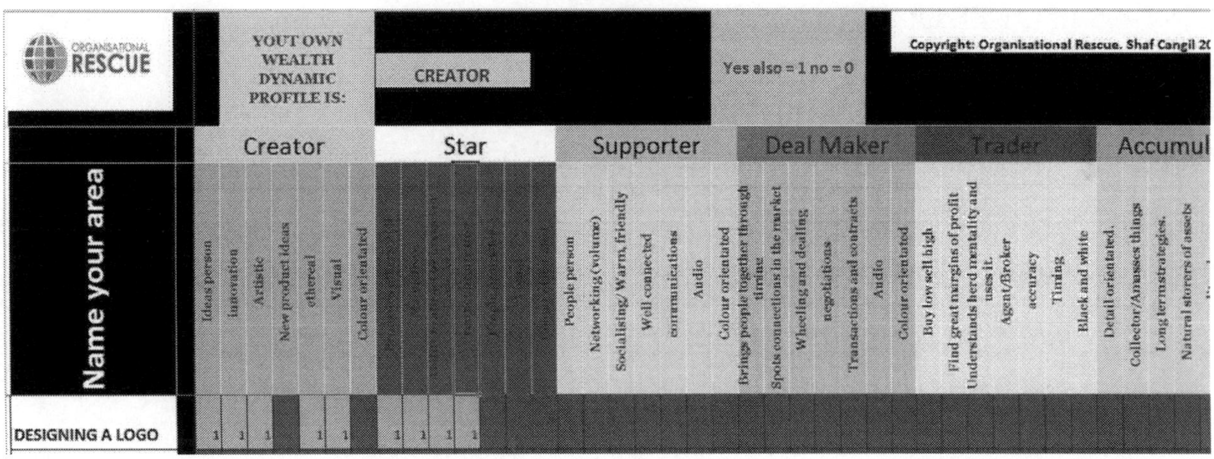

Here is one we did already:

Where the tasks align with 5 or more attributes of the profile above AND it matches your profile, you are told that it is YOUR FLOW. You can choose to take this task yourself. If you are busy you can find another Creator to do this task.

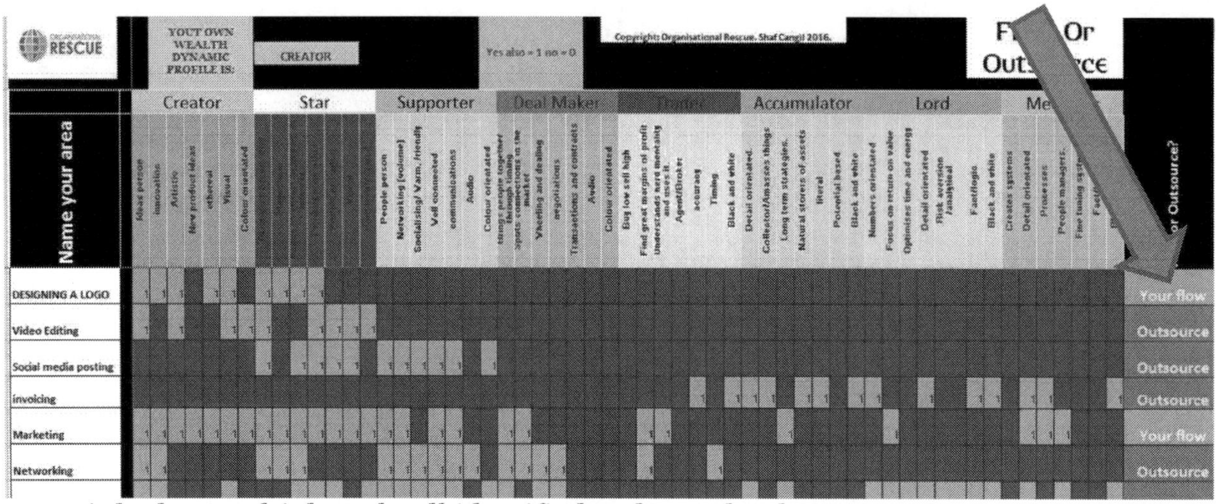

Let's look at multiple tasks all identified and see what happens...

So now with all the tasks filled in, you can see what matches YOUR FLOW and you can choose to do these tasks.

Those that do not match, you can outsource.

But that's not all the Flow or Outsource Engine does...

The engine even tells you which profile to outsource TO AS WELL.

At the far end of the table...

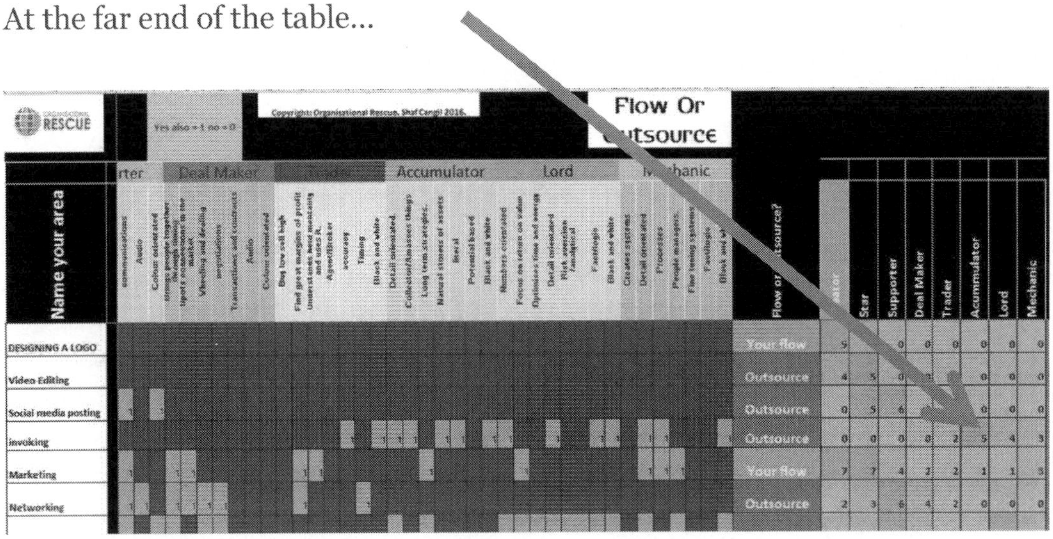

You will see another section that gives a green box as to what profile best matches that task, if it is to be outsourced eg: _Invoicing_ best **outsourced** to an _Accumulator_ indicated with a green cell.

Develop

Now:

1. Take the 'Flow or Outsource Engine' and insert the tasks you want vertically in the Name your area section.
2. Then go horizontally and give a '1' for all the attributes you think they need.
3. Set your own profile at the top. Click on the box to get the drop down button. Select.

Test

Select that tasks you are inflow in and are happy with taking on...
Outsource the other tasks.

Evaluate

Do you feel that you can find out what tasks to outsource and which to do yourself?

What have I discovered?

1. I have identified the characteristics of the tasks in my business according to its attributes.
2. I have identified exactly what tasks in my business are best for me to outsource and best for me to do myself.

ORGANISATIONAL
RESCUE

Dynamo Energy Task
https://www.geniusu.com/my-genius-test

Planning an Event (Didi Dimitrova Suggestion)

Objective:

1. To understand how to set up an event for your business.
2. To fashion the perfect event.

Identify

Events are one of the best ways to get your company noticed and work in a collaborative fashion with like-minded businesses.

First think of WHY you are creating this event. The purpose for gathering many business people and what you want them to come away with. It's all very well thinking about what YOU want to come away with however it is important that there is some congruency with your own business mission and the message this event will say about you and your future vision (see Future Vision Practical Worksheet P.20).

Let's examine this in detail and add your reasons:

Analyse

YOUR FUTURE VISION AND YOUR EVENT:

POINTS TO CONSIDER	YOUR ANSWERS.
What are your own personal values that energise you?	

What do you see happening around you and because of you in business?	
What are your strengths and how can you use them?	
What are your areas of weakness that you will need help with and can you get this?	
Do you feel stressed, obliged or frustrated when thinking about what you will be providing?	
How is the event going to be of value to others? (Identify 5 ways it is of value to others)	
Is it a congruent direction with what your business stands for?	
Are you aligned right now this this direction or is this a divergent opportunity?	
Does this event excite you in its entirety?	
Can you quantify the take away of this event for your Target Market?	
Would you enjoy the event regardless of reaching the target?	
Would you dedicate the time to it, even if you didn't breakeven?	
When you talk about this event do people comment on how excited	

YOU become?	
What do you want from this event?	

If you have answered the list above and still feel it is a good idea to create an event then let us beak down the steps.

Design

Here are some steps you should be doing in order to create an event.

Event planning	What to do	Have done it (& Notes).
Make mindmap or spider diagram of the event.	You can use pencil and paper or you can use this free downloadable software to plan clearly.(Freemind http://freemind.sourceforge.net/wiki/index.php/Download) Try to add at least 5 spokes radiating out and add a sub set of the main event concept in each. Eg: If you are creating an event for **Empowering Women** http://www.unwomen.org/en/partnerships/businesses-and-foundations/womens-empowerment-principles You would research this and add the title to the centre then think of at least 5 areas that you know are the current top talking points surrounding it. 1. Establish high-level corporate leadership for gender equality **('How to Break The Female Glass ceiling')** 2. Treat all women and men fairly at work—respect and support human rights and non-discrimination **('Gender Tender Workplaces')**	

	3. Ensure the health, safety and well-being of all women and men workers **('Mindful Workspaces.')** 4. Promote education, training and professional development for women **("Running up corporate Ladders, in your tights!')** 5. Implement enterprise development, supply chain and marketing practices that empower women **('Find and use The Old Girls Network')** 6. Promote equality through community initiatives and advocacy **('Man's world, but it would be nothing without a woman or a girl!')** 7. Measure and publicly report on progress to achieve gender equality- **('Hidden in full view')**	
Expand the map	Take each area now and spend one hour researching each one. Add branches to the mindmap with key points until you have at least 3 branches in each.	
Experts in each field	Contact your circle and find an expert in the top 5 fields that you have lots of data for. Put feelers out and mention that you are having an event for Empowering women and it will have these 5 points. Ask which they would like to talk on.	
Location, Location, Location	One of the most important aspects is to have a location that is easy to get to and based in a very favourable area. Large hotels hold events with lush surrounds and the ability for participants to stay overnight if they so wish. Check out 5 hotels and look at their prices and what is included with that. • Do they provide coffee/refreshments? • Sandwiches? • Projector? • Technician? • Sound equipment?	

	• Laptop? • seating around tables, in rows, • What capacity would you be looking at? • How long is it for a day or a weekend? • How far in advance do you have to book up? • Is there a refund policy? • How soon do you have to pay all the cost? • Available dates? • How much?	
Dates.	In any event it is a great idea to have a theme that the event can maximise. If it is in January you might have a New Year's Resolution event with your main topic. here are a few other ideas: • January: New year's resolutions • February: St Valentine's day • March: International Women's day • April: St Georges day • May: Global Campaign for education action • June: World ocean day. • July: World population day • August: Water week • September: International Day of peace. • October: Black history month • November: Stress awareness day • December: World Aids day https://www.awarenessdays.co.uk/ Awareness days [http://www.clareflorist.co.uk/special dates.asp Claire florists special dates 2016-17] http://projectbritain.com/specialdays.htm British Life & Culture Awareness Days and Weeks.	
Sponsors	You may be able to get some sponsorship from businesses that would advertise their banners in your event. They might have a	

	representative in your foyer too where they could be promoting their own business without taking part in the event itself. https://www.youtube.com/watch?v=mY9jeB0bJnw Questions: Who wants access to your target audience? Who would be willing to pay for them? https://www.youtube.com/watch?v=puOuFjIVsGg See if companies will consider donating some inventory or time instead of pure cash. ('Donations in Kind'). Use that partnership to approach other companies and make them think they are missing out. If you can, use the Wealth Dynamics profile as leverage. https://www.youtube.com/watch?v=fdmzZ9Ps7As http://www.wikihow.com/Seek-Sponsorships Find 3 related businesses that would benefit from the partnership and event. Who are they?	
Budget and target	Here is where you start to calculate the actual monetary revenue the event could generate and where you should be cutting back or spending more on. Where are the revenue streams for you? Watch these short clips. https://www.youtube.com/watch?v=Es4-t3ih8BA [Income activator]	

	https://www.youtube.com/watch?v=fXbhAr4u0yo [online revenue generator, Income activator] https://www.youtube.com/watch?v=nhSmTwiTfNk [Pay per click ads. Income activator] https://www.youtube.com/watch?v=Ur8V3fKME6s [Creating your own product line. Income activator] Can you have some t-shirts, caps, trinkets or mugs created to give away at events to potential business partners or colleges? Have you got permission to use images from the event? Do you have it designed? Can you give 'Signage' space to related businesses at your event in exchange for payment? Locate publications and place ads well in advance. Which publications have you found? Do the math and find your breakeven point. Work to find the sales you need to create the target profit you set. Related books: Gorilla marketing: https://www.amazon.co.uk/Guerrilla-Marketing-Cutting-edge-strategies-century/dp/0749928115	
Key Revenue Streams used in Businesses	https://www.youtube.com/watch?v=Je2nVCtimbk [Potential] Questions: • What asset sales do you have to sell to generate cash? • What fee have you set for speakers? • Do you have subscription fees for ongoing membership connected to the event or experience? • What leasing assets could you provide for the event? • Do you have any licensing options?	

	• Where could you add brokerage fees for facillitation transactions at the event? • What advertising fees can you get from advertising relevant products at the event?	
Timeline	Build a simple timeline in excel. This will allow you to place all the elements in logical order and thus give you a pace that you will need towork at. Set the date of the event on it and then break down all tasks equally into this. We would advise removing all dates you know you would not be available to work first.	
Promotional videos	Make a simple You Tube clip to promote your event. https://www.youtube.com/watch?v=VZzBym2_X0w [Nate Woodbury: Making a promotional video] https://www.youtube.com/watch?v=_7HVhnSYX1Y [eHow: Promoting your event] Questions: Have you found the Social Media your target market uses to place the event? What media have you decided to use?	
Recurring event	Is this a recurring event? You should make sure that if it is you make this clear to the target market and speakers. Advance bookings are always best and you may consider adding a discount too.	
After event wind down	You may consider having an after event section that is an extra to promote further business opportunities. Networking over sparking wine and coffee goes down well and can give you time to make sure everyone has had a good time and you can gather feedback to improve your next event.	

The main thing is to create momentum for the event in the social media of your target audience.

You may build a Facebook group or use Facebook ads, get people excited through emails and newsletters and even attract the media.

Develop

Find out your perfect combination of speakers by checking the potential cash flow from each possible source and matching against your target.

Test

Do you think that you can identify and increase the more challenging speakers that have large attendances at their meet ups? Which type of payment method works best for your business, speakers and clients?

What can you update to improve?

Evaluate

Do you feel that you have some better options for your event to increase the possibility of completed targets overall?

What have I discovered?

1. I understand how to set up an event for my business.
2. I have fashioned the perfect event.

*** Thank you to Didi Dimitrova of DD Business Solutions Ltd for providing this problem for our Practical Worksheet solutions!**

ORGANISATIONAL
RESCUE

E-Loyalty Cards

(Jo Fellowes Suggestion)

Blaze Energy Task
https://www.geniusu.com/my-genius-test

Objective:

1. To understand that stickiness can be enhanced via loyalty schemes like e-cards.
2. To create my own e-loyalty cards that brings new clients through word of mouth.

Identify

When a business has a client base that depends on referrals and word of mouth, new signups can be slow and unreliable even if you are giving incredible value for money.

That's why large companies like Costas, Starbucks, Tesco's, Sainsbury's and many others use a loyalty card scheme that is guaranteed to bring back customers and encourage new ones too, as well as providing you with ample data for your research so you can build suitable programs and products that fit your target audience specifically.

Electronic cards on mobile devices are replacing the plastic card.

Let's take a look at one specific e-loyalty card and how it works for you.

Analyse

Digital loyalty card schemes have been gaining popularity because they are kept on your mobile device. It's possible to send text messages to encourage those that are nearby to pop in. Alternatively special promotions can be texted direct to them. By using a scan-able code they can instantly be credited stamps and data can be uploaded directly to be viewed.

You design your own stamp card for your campaign and then copy the unique QR code to your website or social media so the user can get a card immediately.

We like the look of Loopy Loyalty Cards at https://loopyloyalty.com/. They are particularly exciting as with unlimited campaigns you get 5000 cards so you can create special offers when you want for how long you want and for what you want.

Design

Let's break down your next steps here:

You will need your logo, corporate colours (brand colours) a few images that you can use for free (see FreeDigitalPhotos at http://www.freedigitalphotos.net/. As long as you add a copyright acknowledgement near the image you use, it's free too!)

Sign up for free and then get busy creating the design setting the number of stamps you wish, the colours the images and the QR Code.

Develop

Go to the website at: https://loopyloyalty.com/.

Test

Try out this e-loyalty scheme for at least 3 months and see how it affects your business. Set a profit target to achieve in 3 months and work out how many more customers would bring that in. Use this as a SMART goal. Remember to take a measure of your traffic and sales before and after the use of the card in order to make real accurate assessment of effectiveness.

Evaluate

Do you feel that you have increased stickiness to your business now as a result of using the e-loyalty card scheme? In what way?

What have I discovered?

1. I understand that stickiness can be enhanced via loyalty schemes like e-cards.
2. I can create my own e-loyalty card that brings new clients through word of mouth.

*** Thank you to Jo Fellowes for providing the problem for our Practical Worksheet solutions!**

ORGANISATIONAL
RESCUE

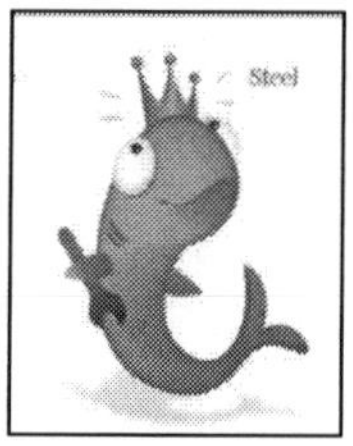

Steel Energy Task
https://www.genius u.com/my-genius-test

Collect and categorise your assets

(Phil Heeley Suggestion)

Objective:

1. To understand how to collect and categorise your assets.
2. To direct customers to the right asset for their purposes.

Identify

Image courtesy of Danilo Rizzuti at FreeDigitalPhotos.net

Every business should have a clear definition of their assets for sale.

Here we will collect and categorise your assets and by doing this help your customer understand the boundaries and choose the right asset for their purposes.

This can provide a personalised platform per customer.

Analyse

We start by collecting and categorising your current assets into three distinct **packages**. We use three for simplicity, where the current marketplace is used to being given a mid-range option, a more affordable or free option and a high end customised option.

Image courtesy of stockimages at FreeDigitalPhotos.net

Benefits and limitations

One asset type will offer you Word of Mouth branding and advertising thus saving you placing adverts in magazines.

Although these people may never buy from you, by sharing your details in their social media and giving testimonials, they will gain the attention of the next level of customer for you.

The next asset type could be a payable mixture of automated and one to one options like webinars, or books or perhaps Skype sessions with multiple people.

Image courtesy of Master isolated images at FreeDigitalPhoto.net

The last asset type would be those that would never pay any less than the top dollar and expect great return. These you would have customised packages for.

Image courtesy of digitalart at FreeDigitalPhotos net

Allow your clients to choose their own option.

Just as in the market place each person has their own budget and will use that comfortably; each will have a desire to stretch beyond their budget.

Provide a consultation with each to help them decide which way to choose.

Provide financing options too.

Now we have a better idea of our products and clients, let's look at how they actually fit together...

Image courtesy of Ambro at FreeDigitalPhotos net

Design

Next to each of the listed branches add your answer

Image courtesy of Ambro at FreeDigitalPhotos net

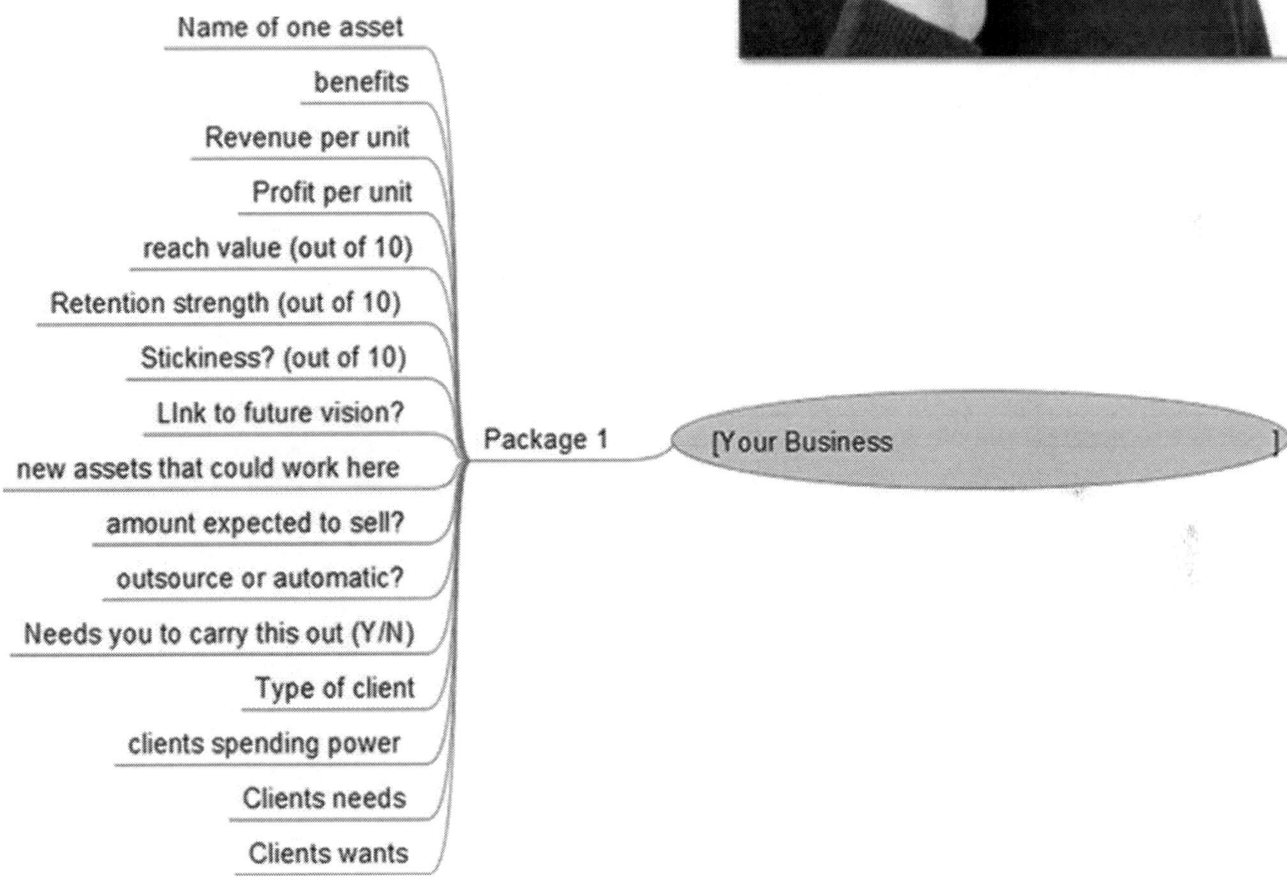

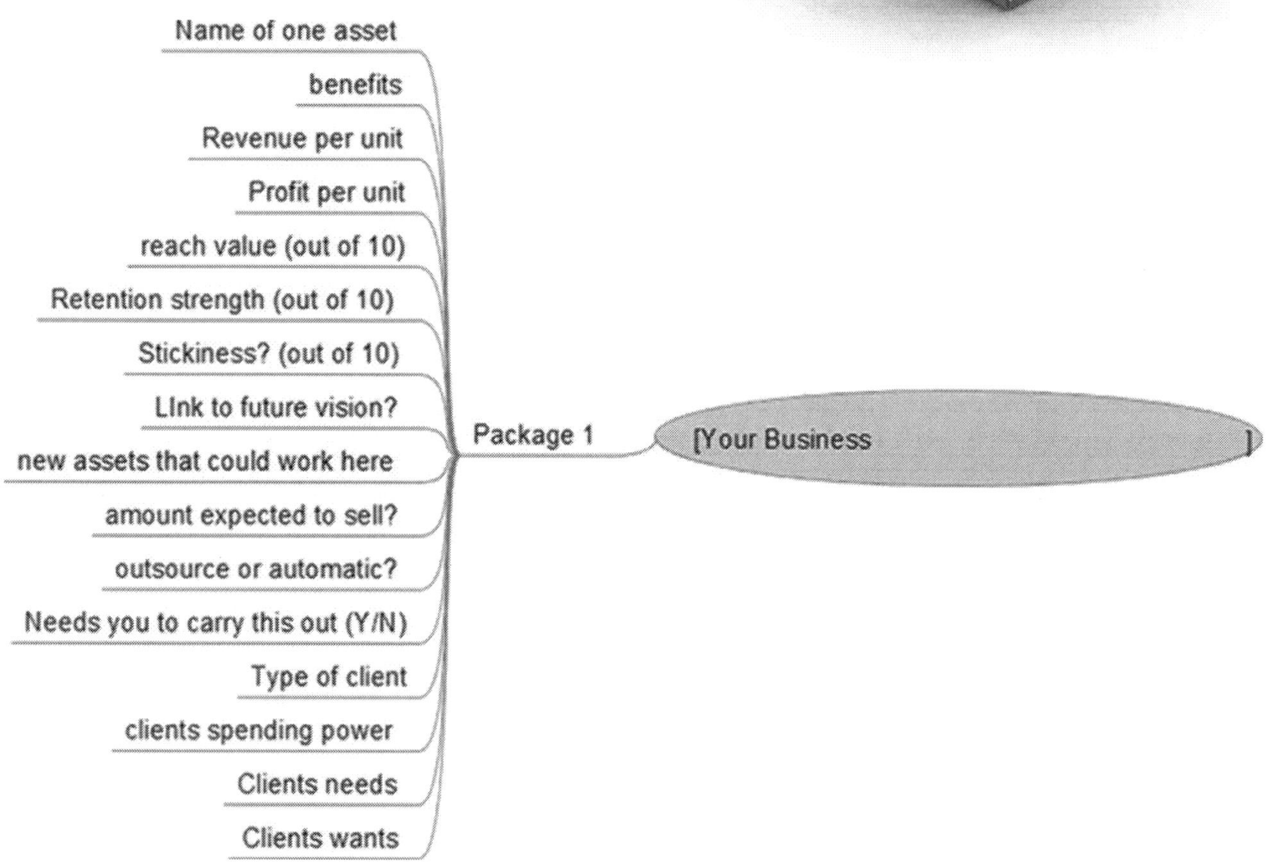
Name of one asset
benefits
Revenue per unit
Profit per unit
reach value (out of 10)
Retention strength (out of 10)
Stickiness? (out of 10)
LInk to future vision?
new assets that could work here
amount expected to sell?
outsource or automatic?
Needs you to carry this out (Y/N)
Type of client
clients spending power
Clients needs
Clients wants
Package 1
[Your Business]

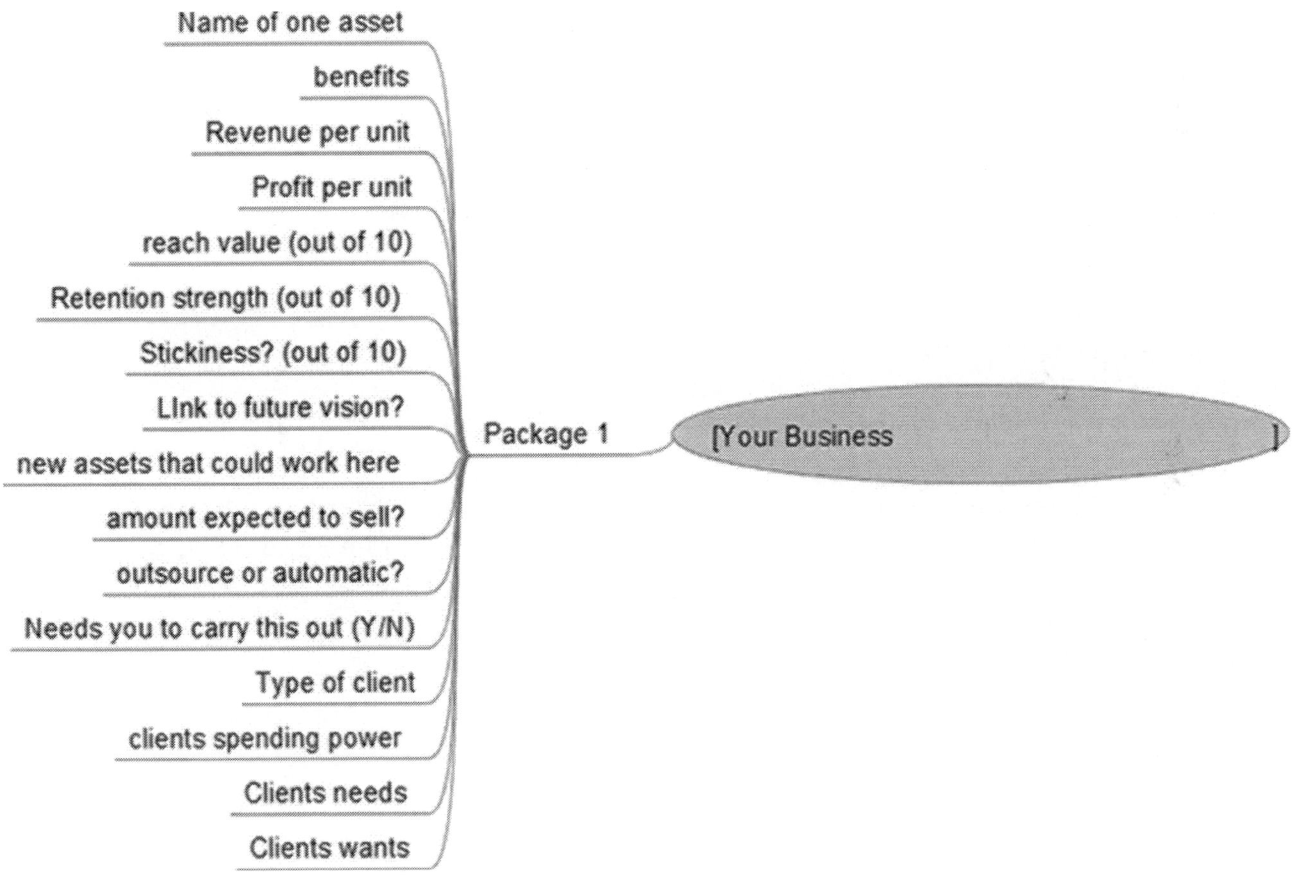
Name of one asset
benefits
Revenue per unit
Profit per unit
reach value (out of 10)
Retention strength (out of 10)
Stickiness? (out of 10)
LInk to future vision?
new assets that could work here
amount expected to sell?
outsource or automatic?
Needs you to carry this out (Y/N)
Type of client
clients spending power
Clients needs
Clients wants
Package 1
[Your Business]

How you use these packages are important too.
This is a simplified flowchart of **how** to use them.

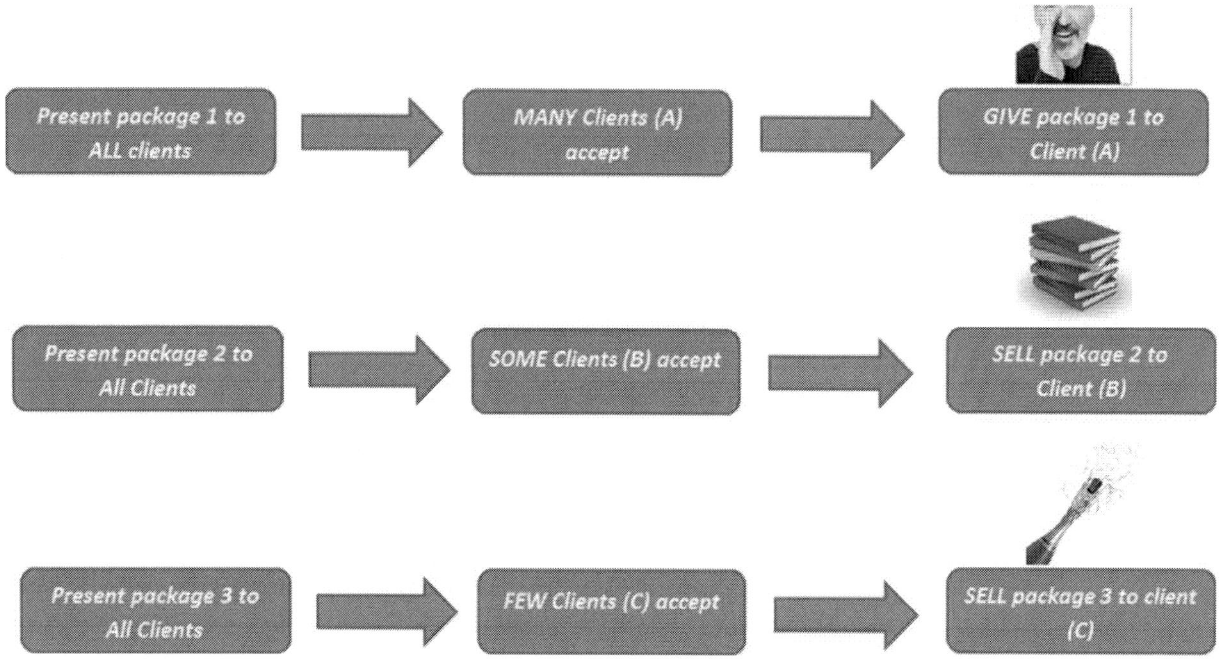

Develop

- Now we have the structure and the game plan we will need to keep refining and updating the 3 packages. This is normal.
- Keep the end user in mind, not your own desires. Your desire should be to keep the customer returning and getting great value while you make your targets.
- If you follow the flowchart you should be able to now create a simple online test to help your customers select the right package.
- Here is a free online quiz that you can use to do this.

https://www.surveymonkey.co.uk/

Test

- Try out three packages on a sample section or for a trial period for a month.
- Note the changes in sales per month and see if this is beneficial to you.
- Change one of the packages slightly and see if the next month this makes any difference. This is A/B Testing and is the way companies upgrade their offers.

Evaluate

Do you feel that you understand how to collect and categorise your assets now? Do you feel that you can direct customers to the right packages? What changes worked for your company?

What have I discovered?

1. I understand how to collect and categorise my assets.
2. I can direct customers to the right asset for their purposes.

*** Thank you to Phil Heeley for providing this problem for our Practical Worksheet solutions!**

ORGANISATIONAL
RESCUE

Automated Advertising

(Ida Ahmet Suggestion)

Tempo Energy Task
https://www.geniusu.com/my-genius-test

Objective:

1. To understand how to set value in automate advertising messages on a regular basis via various social media outlets.
2. To create an automated plan to do this.

Identify

Warning! Make sure the products you select to sell are items that your target market will definitely buy!

Automating regular notifications that highlight the value and benefits of your products on social media has been made simple by software that allows you to set up your series of ads and shoot them off from one point of origin.

We assume that you have a list of products that you are confident will sell and we also assume that you have a good idea of the expendable income your target market spends on a regular basis.

Let's also assume you have a shopping site online. If not try: https://www.tipsandtricks-hq.com/how-to-easily-create-a-simple-wordpress-store-online-for-free-4565

When sending out repeat adverts consider using: Hootsuite https://hootsuite.com/en-gb Sendible http://sendible.com/ or Buffer https://buffer.com/

By using one of these automated notification systems you can line up a series of tweets and posts in order, so it looks like you are online 24/7. You can set special ads on certain dates like St Valentine's Day or Mothering Sunday to encourage sales all without doing another thing!

Let's look at how you can use these notifications productively.

Analyse

There are many online you tube clips showing you ***how*** to install and use systems which is not our intent here, such as:

Hootsuite.

https://www.youtube.com/watch?v=t9vs0PfgXsc For bulk uploading see this: https://www.youtube.com/watch?v=AZHsAlGyxV8

Sendible

https://www.youtube.com/watch?v=k7jLsX3hYVs

or Buffer

https://www.youtube.com/watch?v=v94VSDYUeKE

but it IS our aim to show you a few ideas you can do with them.

Send Images

At any one time the best social media to advertise on may change. Using a highly illustrative platform with regular appealing images works better than any text based notifications. Always do your research. Find existing popular image posts in that social media that already have a strong similarity to your products. This means a little research finding the right ones. The aim is to assist their followers to become more aware of what YOU have to offer them too.

Once found, can add comments making sure you have added details to your own site in your profile there not direct on the post.

- **Get 10 great images that are either your own exclusively or eye catching and copyright free. Try for a more personalised option rather than from generic stock online.**

- **Text Words**

Think 'catchy' for titles on blog posts. Newspaper headlines are tantalising for a reason. Offer your ideas in the posts but holdback on an absolute antidote. If you encourage debate, you get noticed! Next thing you know, they will be checking out your profile and website!

- **Create 10 awesome topics from the coming months to write about and set an awesome headline for each.**

Post Freebies

Freebies are always welcome too. If it solves a problem for the user, that is. But don't just give away stuff without thinking. Have a hook on them that will make people search you out for more.

- **Think of 5 freebies that you can giveaway that cost you absolutely nothing that have a hook.**

Send You Tube Clips

If you can make your own GREAT, (CamStudio is a great free tool to record your desktop http://camstudio.org/) however if you can't, then researching You Tube clips with high subscribers or likes on areas that closely match your own products will allow you to tap into the audience of others. Just comment (It's not acceptable to add your own link but if you make a real good comment of value, people will want to know who you are and will search your profile and you can add your site details there). Just adding your own link is tacky and a real turn off!

- ***Make 5 videos that illustrate the solution your product provides for the buyer. Make sure they are less than 2 minutes long. People have short attention spans. If you send out the latest news on your products from other people that is just as useful to you! Use your Mobile phone for that real authentic hands on feel, which is all the rage now.***

Techniques you might like to try to capture attention throughout the year.

By linking your products and sales to events throughout the year, you appear to be on the ball and very with it. Offering discounts at these times can help you gather sales and building up to them over time can be automated as well. Tension helps sales!

- ***What 5 main events per year can you see that give your target market a reason to buy your products?***

Design

Let's examine the techniques you might like to try to capture attention throughout the year.

Techniques	What you will use.	Times of the year to send out.
What 5 main events per year can you see that give your target market a reason to buy your products?	1 2 3 4 5	
Get 10 great images that	1	

are either your own exclusively or eye catching and copyright free relating to those events. *Try for a more personalised option rather than from generic stock online.*	2 3 4 5 6 7 8 9 10	
Create 10 awesome topics from the coming months to write about (That's 2 per event). *Create an awesome headline for each.*	1 2 3 4 5 6 7 8 9 10	
Think of 5 freebies that you can giveaway relating to the events and your products that cost you absolutely nothing that have a hook. (PDF reports, downloadable price lists, videos)	1 2 3 4 5	
Make 5 videos (1 per event) that illustrate an awesome solution your product makes for the buyer. *Add urgency and a deadline. (Early bird offer).*	1 2 3 4 5	

Develop

This is the implementation stage where you will begin to develop the resources mentioned above then start to roll it out.

Take your time over a couple of weeks to gather these first. Do not take too long. This is a work in progress and you will make some mistakes along the way.

The idea is not to be perfect, the idea is to make a decision and act on it. When you test and evaluate the results you can then start again and improve until you have a real set program that is super accurate.

Test

A great way to test is to check the flow to your site and where it's coming from. Google analytics is a superb tool to do that. https://www.Google.co.uk/analytics/

Here's a clip on how to use it

https://www.youtube.com/watch?v=8KODFoR8DlA

Evaluate

Do you feel that you understand how to set value in your advertising so that people will look for you instead of you chasing them? Do you have a plan you can automate now and a platform to do this in?

What have I discovered?

1. I understand how to set value in automate advertising messages on a regular basis via various social media outlets.
2. I have created an automated plan to do this.

*** Thank you to Ida Ahmet for providing this problem for our Practical Worksheet solutions!**

ORGANISATIONAL RESCUE

Special thanks:

My deepest thanks go to the following for agreeing to contribute freely to this book and sharing their time.

- Daniel Priestly
- Patrick Bet David
- Jon Masters
- Justin Farquhar
- Didi Dimitrova
- Phil Heeley
- Jo Fellowes
- Ida Ahmet
- Sonia Czernik
- Pascal J Petit
- Eric Solot

Terms and Conditions:

Organisational Rescue does not provide Support or Accountability options with worksheets. They are a one off plan to give entrepreneurs a guide to follow towards their given goals and their use and consequences are the responsibility of the user only. Users agree to follow given advice correctly. Users agree that Organisational Rescue cannot be held responsible for any result of advice suggested, especially but not exclusively, in cases where it is suspected that given advice is not adhered to. Organisational Rescue endeavours to give you the best in advice and systems according to their knowledge at all times. They reserve the right to adapt these at any time. Where the user refuses to accept full responsibility for using the worksheets they should immediately refrain from doing so.

Copyright: You agree not to share worksheets or systems without the express permission of Organisational Rescue. Contribution and suggestions towards the Practical Worksheets is purely on the basis that the solution is created. It does not invoke any rights to books or further use of the solution created by the suggestor.

ABOUT THE AUTHOR

Shaf Cangil was born in Highbury and Islington on 21st October 1964 on a Wednesday at 4pm at 27 Orpingley Road as school children came home from school.

She has enjoyed being a student at Laycock Primary School, Barnsbury Girls School (Where she fell in love with the green command prompt of the BBC Micro at lunch times) The Islington Sixth form centre, fell in love with the Sinclair ZX81, became a Fine Art Watercolourist entrepreneur, with pictures in films such as Mrs. Doubtfire, became a mum then a games programmer with her own software company producing e-learning software for schools, then a teacher helping school kids appreciate how the real world works and all the way through was learning how to learn and how to share that knowledge.

She knows the meaning of sacrifice and patience and above all being organised.

90993002R00089

Made in the USA
Columbia, SC
12 March 2018